NO

400

FAMOUS

ATHEISTS

and

AGNOSTICS

Plus 60

INFAMOUS THEISTS!

This book is a tribute to all the men and
women, past, present and future who dare
to break free of all the old, traditional,
religious dogma and who choose to be and
do good... simply for goodness sake...not for
the hope of god's rewards in heaven or
for the fear of punishment in hell,
but just because it feels right.

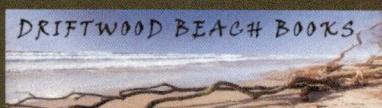

ALSO BY MIKE NEWELL
"370 Wildly Talented
GAYS, BISEXUALS
LESBIANS AND THESPIANS !"

"San Clemente California
Spanish Village By The Sea"

"More Than 10,000 Spanish Words
You Didn't Know You Knew"

"¡Más de 10,000 Palabras en Inglés
Que No Sabías Que Ya Sabías!"

Publisher

DRIFTWOOD BEACH BOOKS

mikenewell@NetHere.com

ISBN - 10: 1-46367-201-2
ISBN - 13:978-1-46367-201-0

Library of Congress Control Number 201193352

ATHEISTS and AGNOSTICS

HOPEFULLY
BOOKS LEAD TO KNOWLEDGE
KNOWLEDGE LEADS TO WISDOM
WISDOM LEADS TO ATHEISM
ATHEISM LEADS TO
WORLD PEACE
HOPEFULLY

Atheists and agnostics are among
the largest minorities worldwide
and as the number of religious people diminishes
more and more non-believers and free thinkers are
coming out of the closet and daring to own
that once dirty word
ATHEISM!
In the Beginning, Man Created God

Douglas Adams

1951-2001 aged 51
Born in Cambridge, England
Writer and Dramatist
Famous for "The Hitchhiker's
Guide to the Galaxy" etc

"I really do not believe there is a god.
I see not a shred of evidence
to suggest that there is one.
It mystifies me that otherwise
intelligent people take it seriously"

John Adams

1735-1826 aged 91

Born in Quincy, Massachusetts

Champion of Independence in 1776

2nd President of The United States 1797-1801

Interestingly, he and Thomas Jefferson of course,
both signed the Declaration of Independence on
4th July 1776—both died on 4th July 1826!
Exactly fifty years later!

"This would be the best of all possible worlds
if there were no religion in it. The Government of
the United States is in no sense founded on the
Christian religion.
The Divinity of Jesus Christ is made a
convenient cover for absurdity"

Edward Albee

Born 1928 in Washington, DC
Pulitzer Prize Winning
Playwright and Atheist
"Who's Afraid of Virginia Woolf"
etc

He had a strong
religious experience
in church when he was four ...
and from that moment on he
began to lose his faith.

Ayaan Hirsi Ali

Born 1969 in Mogadishu, Somalia
Lived in Saudi Arabia, Ethiopia,
Kenya and since 1992, in Holland

Dutch Writer, Politician,
Feminist and Ex-Muslim.

Married Scottish Historian

Niall Ferguson in 2011

"Islam is a backward religion,
incompatible with democracy.
Women can be stoned to death,
homosexuals beaten and
those who renounce their
religion like me, killed"

Dave Allen

1936-2005 aged 69

Born in Dublin, Ireland

Very Popular Irish Comedian
In England, Canada and
Australia

"Whatever we cannot easily
understand, we call God;
this saves much wear & tear
on the brain tissues!

"I'm a practicing...
what you might call...
atheist, thank god!"

Fred Allen

1894-1956 aged 62

Born in Cambridge, Massachusetts

American Comedian

Star of Radio, TV and Films

"Most of us spend the
first six days of each week
sowing wild oats, then
we go to church on Sunday
and pray for a crop failure!
The first time I sang in the church choir
two hundred people changed their
religion!"

Steve Allen

1921-2000 aged 79
Born in New York City
Award Winning TV Personality
Musician, Comedian, Actor and Writer.
Wrote over 14,000 Songs!
"It's not hardness of heart or evil passions
that drive individuals to atheism,
but intellectual honesty.
No tyrant has ever been guilty of the crimes,
massacres and atrocities
attributed to the Bible's Deity
Millions of Germans had absolute faith in
Hitler.
Millions of Russians had absolute faith in
Stalin.
Millions of Chinese had absolute Faith in
Mao.
Billions have absolute faith in imaginary
Gods"

Woody Allen

Born 1935 in New York City

Screen Writer, Film Director

Actor, Author, Comedian

Jazz Musician and Playwright

"Not only is God dead, but just try to find
a plumber on weekends"

"If only God would give me some clear
sign. Like making a large deposit in my
name in a Swiss Bank"

"I believe there's something out there
watching us. Unfortunately, it's the
Government"

"If God exists, I hope he has
a good excuse"

Abu'l-Ala-Al-Ma'arri

973-1058 aged 85
Born in M'arra, Syria
Blind Syrian Arab Poet
Philosopher and Writer

"The world holds two classes of men;
Intelligent men
without religion
and
religious men
without intelligence"

Natalie Angier

Born 1958 in The Bronx, New York
Pulitzer Prize Winning
Science Writer with the
New York Times

"Today, nothing seems as despised, illicit and
un-American as atheism...So I'll out myself.
I'm an Atheist. I don't believe in God, Gods,
Godlets or any sort of higher power beyond the
universe itself, which seems quite high and
powerful enough to me. I don't believe in life
after death...reincarnation...or any miracles,
but the miracle of life and consciousness...
I'm convinced that the world was shaped
by the hand of evolution,
through natural selection.
Atheism to me means an ongoing devotion to
exploration, giving pride of place to evidence"

Jean Anouilh

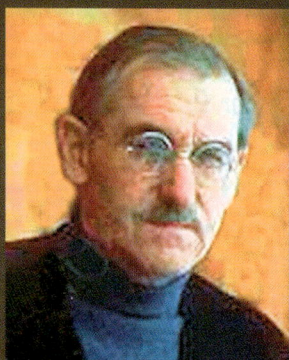

1910-1987 aged 77
Born Near Bordeaux, France
French Dramatist

Best Known for "Antigone"
"Ardele"
and "Ring Round the Moon"

"Every man thinks
god is on his side.
The rich and powerful
know he is"

Saint Thomas Aquinas

1225-1274 aged 49
Born in Roccasecca, Italy
Italian Roman Catholic
Dominican Priest
Philosopher and Theologian

"Clearly the person who accepts the Church as an infallible guide will believe whatever the Church teaches.
Unbelief is the greatest of sins"

Aristophanes

448 BC-385 BC aged 63

Born in Athens, Greece

Athenian Comic Playwright

He Wrote Forty Plays

Eleven of Which Survive Today

"Shrines! Shrines!

Surely you don't believe in the gods!

What's your argument?

Where's your proof?

It is wrong always, everywhere for
anyone to believe anything upon
insufficient evidence"

Aristotle

384 BC-322 BC aged 62
Born in Stagira, Macedonia
Greek Philosopher
Student of Plato and
Teacher of Alexander the Great

"A tyrant must put on the appearance
of uncommon devotion to religion.
Subjects are less apprehensive of illegal
treatment from a ruler whom they
consider pious and god-fearing.
On the other hand,
they do less easily move against him,
believing he has the gods on his side"

Karen Armstrong

Born 1944 in Wildmoor, Worcestershire

Former Roman Catholic Nun

English Author of Books on

History of Religions and

Comparative Religions

"The Christian Right today, has absorbed the
endemic violence in American Society:
they oppose reform of gun laws for example,
and support the death penalty.
They never quote the Sermon on the Mount:
"Love thy Neighbor"
"Judge not lest ye be judged"
but base their xenophobia
and aggressive theology on Revelation"

Lance Armstrong

Born 1971 in Dallas, Texas

Multiple Award Winning

Cyclist, Athlete

and Cancer Survivor

Won the Tour de France <u>Seven</u>

Consecutive Times, 1999 to 2005.

He finally admitted to using

performance enhancing drugs...

like so many Tour de France cyclists did.

"If there was a god
I'd still have both nuts"

Carmen Argibay

Born 1939 in Buenos Aires, Argentina
First Female Member of the
Argentine Supreme Court

'I am a militant atheist and support the right of women to decide about their own bodies. I believe that saying up front who one is and what one thinks is an indication of honesty, which is the first step towards impartiality. My beliefs or lack thereof, should not interfere in the judicial decisions I make"

Isaac Asimov

1920-1992 aged 72

Born in Russia

American Science and
Science Fiction Writer
Professor of Biochemistry

"Properly read, the Bible
is the most potent force
for atheism ever conceived"

Peter Atkins

Born 1940 in Amersham
Buckinghamshire
Writer and Lecturer in
Quantum Mechanics and
Quantum Chemistry at Oxford
Well Known Atheist

"Whereas religion scorns the power
of human comprehension, science
respects it. Religion is a fantasy
and completely empty of
explanatory content.
It is also evil"

Brooks Atkinson

1920-1992 aged 72

Born in Melrose, Massachusetts
Doyen of American Theater Critics
With a Broadway Theater
Named After Him

"People everywhere enjoy believing
things that they know are not true.
It spares them the ordeal of thinking
for themselves and taking
responsibility for
what they know"

Earl Clement Atlee

1883-1967 aged 84

Born in Putney, London

British Labour Prime Minister

1945-1951

Introduced
the National Health Service
and the Welfare State

"I'm one of those people
who are incapable
of religious feeling,
I can't believe in all
the mumbo-jumbo"

Sir David Attenborough

Born 1926 in London
English Naturalist, Writer
Presenter of TV Nature Programs
for Over Fifty Years

"When believers wonder how I can look at
the beauty of the world, like rainbows
and hummingbirds and not be religious ...
I think of a little child in Africa with a
worm burrowing through his eyeball, so I
find it hard to reconcile that with the notion
of a divine, benevolent creator"

W H Auden

1907-1973 aged 66

Born in York, Yorkshire

Anglo-American

Poet, Essayist and Lecturer

"The only reason the Protestants
and Catholics have given up
the idea of universal domination
is because they've realized they
can't get away with it"
BUT NOW ISLAM?

Saint Augustine

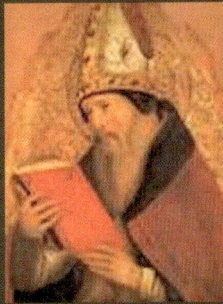

354-430 aged 76

Born in and Lived in

Roman Algeria, North Africa

Latin Speaking

Philosopher & Theologian.

"There is a temptation fraught
with danger. This is the disease of
curiosity which drives one to try and
discover the secrets of nature which are
beyond our understanding, and which
man should not wish to learn"

Sir Francis Bacon

1561-1626 aged 65

Born in London

Philosopher, Scientist, Statesman

Lawyer, One of the Pioneers of Modern

Scientific Thought

"Atheism
inclineth a man to philosophy,
to sense, to natural piety, all of which
are guides to an outward moral virtue.
Truth can never be reached by just
listening to the voice of authority.
Knowledge is power"

Kevin Bacon

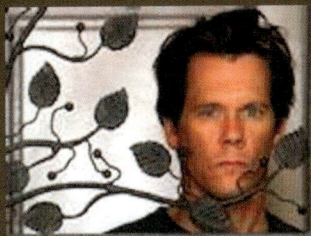

Born 1958 in Philadelphia,

Pennsylvania

Award Winning

American Film and Stage Star

"The arts have it.

Business is the devil's work.

Art and creative expression

are next to godliness"

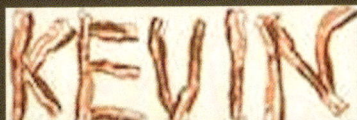

Sheik Abdu Aziz ibn Baaz

1910-1999 aged 89

Born in Riyadh, Saudi Arabia

Saudi Arabia's Supreme
Religious Authority

"The earth is flat,
and anyone who disputes this
is an atheist
who deserves to be punished"

Joan Baez

Born 1941 in Staten Island
New York
Folk Singer, Songwriter
and Activist

"You don't get to choose
how you're going to die.
or when.
You can only decide
how you're going to live,
now"

Russell Wayne Baker

Born 1925 in Morrisonville, Virginia

Pulitzer Prize Winning

Writer, Long-time

New York Times Columnist

"In ruder days, disputes about what constituted a fully qualified Christian often led to sordid quarrels in which the disputants tortured, burned and hanged each other in the conviction that they were the Christian things to do"

Tammy Faye Bakker

1942- 2007 aged 65

Born in International Falls

Minnesota

American Christian Singer

Evangelist, Author, Entrepreneur

Talk Show Host & TV Personality

"I take Him shopping with me,
I say OK, Jesus,
help me find a bargain"

Antonio Banderas

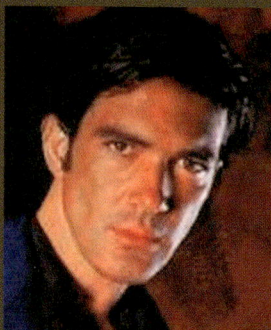

Born 1960 in Malaga, Spain

Spanish and American

Film Star

Director, Producer and Singer

He is an Officer of a Roman
Catholic Religion Brotherhood
in Malaga, Spain.
But he has described himself as
an agnostic.

Javier Bardem

Born 1969 in Las Palmas

Canary Islands

Award Winning

Spanish and American

Film Star

"If I was gay
I'd get married tomorrow...
just to mess with
the church!"

Dan Barker

Born 1949 in Southern California

Christian Preacher for 19 Years

Prominent Atheist Since 1984

"You believe in talking animals, wizards, witches, demons, sticks turning into snakes, food falling from the sky, people walking on water, all sorts of magical, absurd primitive stories, and you say <u>we're</u> the ones who need help?"

Michelle Bachmann

Born 1956 in Waterloo, Iowa

Minnesota Republican Congresswoman

Tea Party Supporter &

Presidential Candidate

"Our beloved Founding Fathers strove

night and day...night and day

to rid this country of slavery"

(IN FACT THEY EACH OWNED MULTIPLE

SLAVES, EVEN HUNDREDS OF SLAVES, AND

THE TRUTH IS OF COURSE, THAT IT WAS THE

16TH PRESIDENT, LINCOLN, WHO EVENTUALLY

SUCCEEDED IN FREEING THE SLAVES...

ALMOST A HUNDRED YEARS LATER !)

...SO IS SHE IGNORANT OR LYING?

...AND WHICH IS WORSE?

Dave Barry

Born 1947 in Armonk,

New York

Pulitzer Prize Winning

Author and Columnist

"People who want to share their religious views with you, almost never want you to share yours with them...but if there really is a God who created the universe with all its glories, and He decided to deliver a message to humanity, He will not use as His messenger, a person on cable TV with a bad hairstyle"

Charles A Beard

1874-1948 aged 74

Born Near Knightstown, Indiana

Leading American Historian

"One of the best ways to get yourself a reputation as a dangerous citizen these days, is to go about repeating the very phrases our Founding Fathers used in the struggle for independence"

Simone de Beauvoir

1908-1986 aged 78

Born in Paris

French Existentialist Writer

Philosopher, Intellectual & Atheist

"It's easier for me to think of a world without a creator than of a creator loaded with all the contradictions of the world...but I cannot be angry at a God in whom I do not believe"

Glenn Beck

Born 1964 in Everett, Washington

Conservative Radio and Ex Fox TV Host

Author and Political Commentator

"Let me give you the words of
George Washington"

"It is impossible to govern a nation
without God and the Bible"

HERE'S WHAT GEORGE WASHINGTON
ACTUALLY SAID ON THE SUBJECT:

"The United States of America
should have a foundation free
from the influence of clergy"

Samuel Beckett

1908-1986 aged 78

Born in Dublin, Ireland

Irish Avant-Garde Writer

Dramatist and Poet

Nobel Prize Winner in 1969

"The bastard!

He doesn't exist!"

Hector Berlioz

1803-1869 aged 66
Born in La Côte-Saint-Andre
Near Lyon, France
French Romantic Composer
most Famous for
Symphonie Fantastique

An atheist, he said;
"Time is a great teacher,
but unfortunately
it kills all its pupils"

Pope Benedict XVI

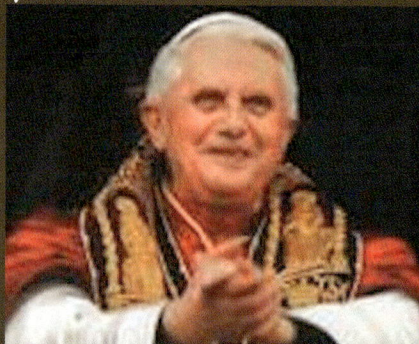

Born 1927 in Marktl, Bavaria

Joseph Ratzinger ex-Nazi Youth

Ex-Archbishop of Munich

"Grant that we may be one
flock and one shepherd"

ONLY SHEEP NEED SHEPHERDS!

Ingmar Bergman

1918-2007 aged 89

Born in Uppsala, Sweden
Swedish Film Writer, Director and
Producer for Film, Stage and TV

Described by Woody Allen as
"Probably the greatest film artist
since the invention of the
moving picture camera"
"I hope I never get so old
I get religious"

Sarah Bernhardt

1844-1923 aged 79

Born in Paris

"The Divine Sarah"

French Actress on Stage

and Early Films

"The most famous actress
the world has ever known"

"Me pray?
Never! I'm an Atheist!"

Dr Andrew Bernstein

Born 1949

American Philosopher,
Educator and Author

"Many argue that Christianity is different from other religions...that it is primarily about love of one's fellow man. However, the Crusades and the Inquisition prove this is not the case. These events were pre-eminently about obedience to authority"

Ambrose Bierce

1842-1913 aged 71

Born in Horse Cave Creek, Ohio

Writer, Journalist, Satirist, Wit

"CLERGYMAN: A man who manages our spiritual
affairs, to better his temporal ones.

INFIDEL: In New York, one who doesn't believe in
Christianity: in Istanbul, one who does.

RELIGION: Explaining to ignorance the
nature of the Unknowable.

SCRIPTURES: The sacred books of our holy religion,
as opposed to the false, profane
writings of all other religions.

Don't believe without evidence.

Treat things divine with marked respect
..don't have anything to do with them.

THEOLOGY: A thing of unreason altogether,
an edifice of assumptions & dreams, a superstructure
without a substructure"

Björk

Born 1965 in Reykjavik,
Iceland
Prize Winning Singer, Songwriter,
Director, Music Producer, Actress
"The human race, we are a tribe,
let's face it, and let's stop all this
religious bullshit. Everybody's
so very exhausted with all the
self-importance of religious
people. Instead of church
we go out into nature.
Nature is our chapel"

Lewis Black

Born 1948 in Silver Spring, Maryland
Award Winning Comedian, Author
Playwright, Social Critic and Actor

"Funny thing about religion, no matter
what you may say, you're going to upset
someone! I'm not a big fan of religion, but
there must be something out there...I call
it Glue. It was all a wonderful story to
distract the desert people from the fact
there was no air conditioning. I'd like
to have faith, but I have thoughts
and thoughts can really mess up
faith, just ask any
Catholic priest"!

Napoleon Bonaparte

1769-1821 aged 52

Born in Corsica

Emperor of France

"Religion is excellent stuff
for keeping the common people quiet.
I would believe any religion that could prove
it had existed since the beginning of the world.
But when I see Socrates, Plato, Mohammed and
Moses, I do not think there is such a one.
All religions owe their origin to man.
If I had to choose a religion, the sun
as the universal giver of life
would be my god"

Pope Boniface VIII

1235-1303 aged 68

Born in Anagni, Papal States

Near Rome, Holy Roman Empire

Pope From 1294 to 1303

Famous for His Feuds With

Dante and Philip IV of France

"There is no more harm in
adultery than in rubbing
one's hands together"
!

Daniel Boorstin

1914-2004 aged 90

Born in Atlanta, Georgia

Historian, Professor

Attorney and Writer

"I have observed that the world
has suffered far less from ignorance
than from pretensions to knowledge.
It is not skeptics and explorers, but
fanatics and ideologues, who menace
decency and progress. No agnostic ever
burned anyone at the stake or tortured
a pagan, a heretic, or an unbeliever"

Mrs Betty Bowers

America's Best Christian
(Fictitious Comedy Character!)

"The actions taken by the New Hampshire Episcopalians, inducting a gay Bishop, are an affront to Christians everywhere. I'm just thankful that the church's founder, Henry VIII, and his wife Catherine of Aragon and Anne Boleyn and Jane Seymour and Anne of Cleves and Katherine Howard and Catherine Parr can't witness this assault on traditional Christian marriages"

David Bowie

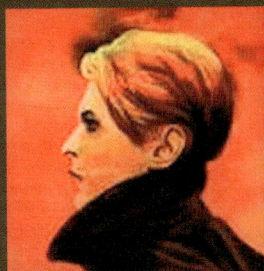

Born 1947 in Brixton, London

English Rock Star Since the Sixties

Also Actor, and Record Producer

"Religion

is for people who fear

Hell

...Spirituality

is for people who have been there.

I'm not quite an atheist,

and it worries me.

..Well I'm almost an atheist.

Give me a couple of months"

Lt. Gen William Boykin

Born in New Bern, North Carolina

Born Again Christian Minister, He was US
Deputy Undersecretary of Defense for Intelligence

"Why is this man

George w Bush in the White House?

The majority of Americans

did not vote for him...

he's in the White house

because GOD put him there"

(WITH HELP FROM KARL ROVE,

JAMES BAKER, KATHERINE HARRIS,

AND THE US SUPREME COURT!)

Ray Bradbury

Born 1920 in Waukegan, Illinois

Science Fiction Writer

Former Baptist

"At the center of religion is love.

I love you and I forgive you.

I am like you and you are like me.

I love all people. I love the world.

I love creating.

Everything in our life

should be based on love"

Johannes Brahms

1833-1897 aged 64

Born in Hamburg, Germany

Distinguished German Composer

and Pianist. Lived in Vienna

Music was Brahms' religion.

He pored over the Bible

but he was a Free Thinker.

Nathaniel Branden

Born 1930 in Brampton, Ontario
Canadian Psychologist and
Writer. Student of Ayn Rand

"Anyone in psychotherapy confronts
every day the devastation wrought by
the teachings of religion. It is a curious
paradox that a doctrine that tells
human beings to regard themselves as
sacrificial animals, has been accepted
as a doctrine representing
benevolence and love of mankind"

Marlon Brando

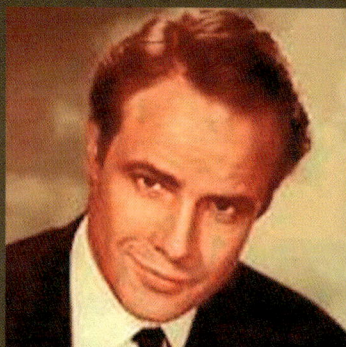

1924-2004 aged 80

Born in Omaha, Nebraska

Fine Stage and Screen Actor

For Over Fifty Years

"I will not swear on God...
because I don't believe in this
nonsense. What I will swear on
is my children and my
grandchildren"

Sir Richard Branson

Born 1950 in Blackheath, London

British Entrepreneur

Adventurer

Dyslexic Billionaire

Atheist Tycoon.

His Virgin Group

has 400 Companies

"There is no convincing

evidence

there is a higher being"

André Breton

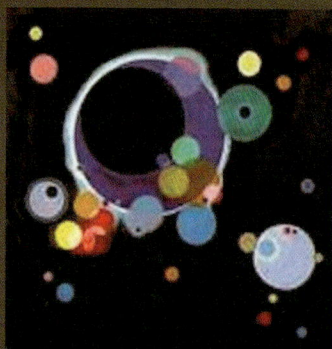

1896-1966 aged 70

Born in Normandy, France

French Writer, Poet

and Surrealist Art Collector

"I have always wagered against God...
I am conscious of having won to the
full. Everything that is doddering,
squint-eyed, vile, polluted and
grotesque is summoned up
for me in that one word:
God!"

Encyclopedia Britannica

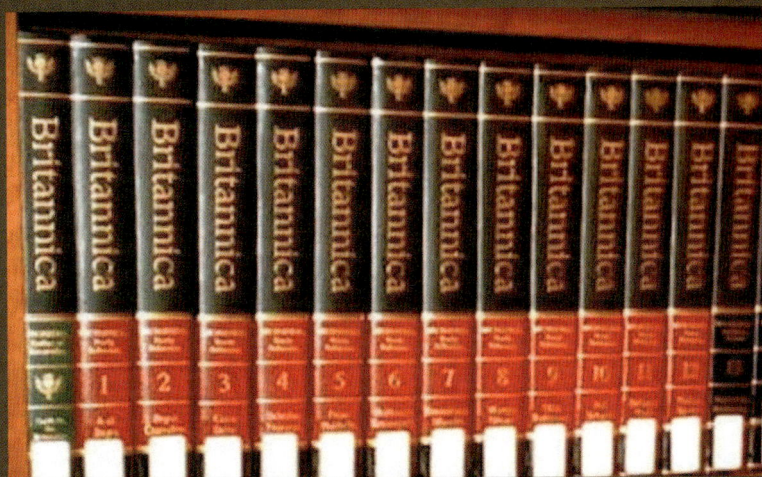

"One of the embarrassing
problems for the
Champions of the Christian
faith was that
not one of the first six
Presidents of the United States
was a an orthodox Christian"

Charlie Brooker

Born 1971 in Reading, Berkshire
British Journalist, Comic Writer
Broadcaster with Savage Wit

"If you want comforting, suck your
thumb. We should be solving problems,
not sticking our fingers in our ears.
From fundamental death cults to
arrogant invasions:
a startling lack of logic unites them.
Cold, clear rational thought is the
most important thing we have;
the one thing that can save us"

Lenny Bruce

1925-1966 aged 41

Born in Mineola, New York.

Comedian, Social Critic and Satirist

He was often charged with using what

then was considered obscene humor

"If Jesus had been killed twenty years

ago, Catholic school children would be

wearing little electric chairs round

their necks instead of crosses. Alright,

let's admit it, we Jews killed Christ,

but it was only for three days"

Bill Bryson

Born 1951 in Des Moines, Iowa

Best Selling Author of Humorous

Travel Books and Other Genre.

Lived for many years in England

Is Chancellor of Durham University

"Think of a problem confronting the

world today.

Disease, poverty, global warming...

if the problem is going to be solved...

it will be by a guy or a woman

with a science degree"

James Buchanan

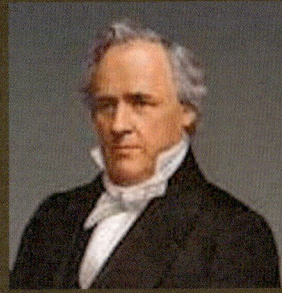

1791-1868 aged 77

Born in a Log Cabin in Cove Gap

Pennsylvania

Democratic

15ᵗʰ President of the United States 1857-1861
Was unable to prevent the Civil War in 1864.
He was succeeded by Abraham Lincoln.

"I have seldom met an intelligent man
whose views were not narrowed and distorted
by religion"

Pearl Buck

1892-1973 aged 81

Born in Hillsboro, West Virginia

First American Woman to be Awarded

the Nobel Prize for Literature

Also the Pulitzer Prize Twice

She Lived Most of Her Life in China

and is Best known for "The Good Earth"

"I feel no need for any other faith than

my faith in the kindness of human

beings. I am so absorbed in the wonder of

the earth and the life upon it that I

cannot think of heaven and angels"

Buddha

563 BC-483 BC aged 80

Born in Nepal, India

Founder of Buddhism

"Do not believe anything simply because it is in your religious books. Do not believe in traditions only because they have been handed down for many generations. Do not believe on the faith of the sages of the past. But after examination, believe what you yourself have tested and found to be reasonable"

Warren Buffett

Born 1930 in Omaha, Nebraska

Billionaire Investor and

Philanthropist

One of the Greatest Investors of all time

One of the world's wealthiest men

Raised Presbyterian

But is now an

Agnostic Rationalist

Who Gave Up Belief in God

at an Early Age

Sandra Bullock

Born 1964 in Arlington, Virginia

Oscar Winning

Hollywood Film Star

Producer and Restaurateur

"People use their faith and their
religion as a banner, they say
I'm a good Christian and I go to
church and this is the way
you should live.. but they
are still sleeping around"

Archie Bunker
(Actor Carroll O'Connor)

Carroll O'Connor

1924-2001 aged 77

Born in Manhattan

He played the role on TV for 13 years!

"Don't ya know what faith is ?
Faith is when you believe
somethin' that nobody in their
right mind would believe!"

Luther Burbank

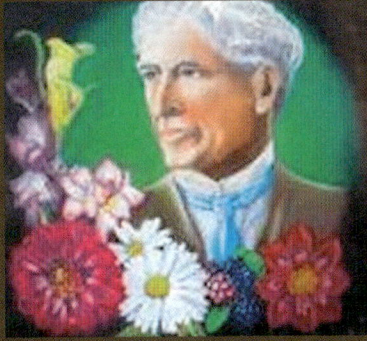

1849-1926 aged 79

Born in Lancaster, Massachusetts

Renowned American Horticulturist

He Developed Countless New Varieties

of Fruits, Vegetables and Flowers

"Most people's religion is what they would <u>like</u> to believe, and very few of them stop to examine its foundations. The idea that a good God would send people to a burning hell, is utterly damnable to me. I don't want anything to do with such a God. Science...has opened our eyes to the vastness of the universe and given us light, truth and freedom from fear, where once was darkness, ignorance and superstition"

Robert Burns

1759-1796 aged 37

Born in Alloway, Scotland

Major Scottish Poet

"Of all Nonsense,
Religious Nonsense
is the most nonsensical.
All religions are auld
wives' fables"

John Burroughs

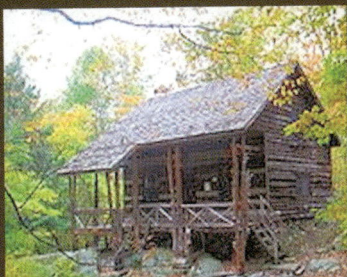

1837-1921 aged 84

Born in a Log cabin in Roxbury,

New York

American Writer, Naturalist

Essayist and Conservationist

"Science has done more for the

development of Western Civilization

in one hundred years,

than Christianity did in

eighteen hundred years.

What remains then, for those who

cannot pray? This alone, & this is enough:

To love virtue, to love truth"

Sir Richard Burton

1821-1890 aged 69

Born in Torquay, Devon

Explorer, Writer, Translator, Soldier

Spy, Diplomat, Poet, Ethnologist

and Linguist. He Spoke 29 Languages!

"The more I study religions,
the more I am convinced
that man never worshiped
anything but himself"

Richard Burton CBE

1925-1984 aged 59

Born in Pontrhydyfen, Wales

Award Winning Actor

On Stage and Screen

"The more I read about man and his
ruthlessness and his murderous soul,
the more I realize he will never
change. The same mistakes,
prejudices, lusts, injustice, … I wish
I could believe in a god of some
kind..but I simply can't"

George H W Bush

Born 1924 in Milton,

Massachusetts

41st President of the United States

"I don't know that atheists
should be considered as citizens,
nor should they be considered
patriots.

This is one nation under God"

WHERE IS IT WRITTEN THAT IF YOU DON'T
LIKE RELIGION, YOU ARE SOMEHOW
DISQUALIFIED FROM BEING AN AMERICAN?
WHAT WAS MARK TWAIN, A RUSSIAN?

George W Bush

Born 1946 in New Haven Connecticut

43rd President of the United States
(Thanks to the Supreme Court,
even though Al Gore got more votes)

"On the issue of evolution,
The <u>verdict</u> is still out
on how God created the Earth"

NOT THE JURY?

Gabriel Byrne

Born 1950 in Dublin, Ireland

Irish Film, Stage and TV Actor,

Film Director and Producer,

Writer and Narrator

"I was sexually abused by

Catholic priests as a child,

so I don't think much of

Catholicism anymore"

Lord Byron

1788-1824 aged 36

Born in London

English Romantic Poet

"Of religion I know nothing,
at least, in its favor. If I am
a fool, it is, at least, a doubting
one; and I envy no one the certainty
of his self-approved wisdom"

George Carlin

1937-2008 aged 71

Born in Manhattan, New York

"I used to believe in God,
until I reached the age of reason.
I would never want to be a member of a group
whose symbol was a guy nailed to two pieces of wood.
When it comes to BS
you really have to stand in awe of the all-time
champion of false promises and exaggerated claims:
Religion. It has to be the greatest BS story ever told.
When it comes to believing in God, I really, really tried,
but the more you look around, the more you
realize...something is wrong here. War, disease,
destruction, death, hunger, filth, poverty, torture,
corruption, crime, the Ice Capades...This is not good work.
If this is the best God can do, I am not impressed.
Results like these do not belong on the résumé of
a Supreme Being"

George Carlin...continued!

"Atheism is a non-prophet organization. Think about it. Religion has actually convinced people that there's an invisible man, living in the sky, who watches everything you do, every minute of every day. And the invisible man has a list of 10 things he does not want you to do. And if you do any of these 10 things, he has a special place, full of fire and smoke and burning and torture and anguish, where he will send you to live and suffer and cry forever and ever 'til the end of time!
But he loves you!"

Andrew Carnegie

1835-1919 Aged 84

Born in Dunfermline, Scotland

He Came From Poverty in Scotland,

to become in America,

the Richest Man in the World

"He that cannot reason is a fool

He that will not is a bigot

He that dare not is a slave

I give money for church organs

in the hope the organ music

will distract the congregation's

attention from the rest of the service

I don't believe in God. My God is patriotism.

Teach a man to be a good citizen and you have

solved the problem. I have not bothered Providence

with my petitions for about forty years"

Jimmy Carr

Born 1945 in London

Comedian, Writer, Actor

Radio and TV Presenter

"When I was a kid
I had an imaginary friend
and I used to think he went
everywhere with me, and that I could
talk to him and that he could hear me
and that he could grant me wishes
and stuff. And then I grew up,
and I stopped going to church"

Richard Carrier

Born 1969 in Orange County

California

Historian, Writer

and Atheist

"I do not believe
there are any gods.
Christians write to me threatening me with
Hell. Strange how they think this
vindicates them and their religion.
Threats are the hallmark
of a wicked creed"

Fidel Castro

Born 1926 in Birán, Cuba

Cuba's President and Former

Communist Revolutionary

"When I was a young boy, my father
taught me to be a good Catholic,
I had to confess at church if ever I had
any impure thoughts about a girl.
That very evening I had to rush to
confess my sin. And the next evening
and the next. After a week,
I decided religion wasn't for me"

Dick Cavett

Born 1936 in Gibbon, Nebraska
Former TV Talk Show Host

"It seems as if the only religion worth having is the simplest possible religion. I'm an almost atheist. As Woody Allen said: "You cannot prove the nonexistence of God; you just have to take it on faith!"

Sir Charlie Chaplin

1889-1977 aged 88

Born in London, England

Comic Film Star and Director

"Religion.

It's given people hope

in a world torn apart by religion.

By simple common sense,

I don't believe in God

I want to play the role of Jesus.

I'm a logical choice. I look the part. I'm a

Jew. And I'm a comedian...And I'm an

atheist, so I could look at the character

objectively. Who else could do that?"

Pierre Charron

1541-1603 aged 62

Born in Paris, France

Theologian, Philosopher,

Lawyer, Writer and Priest

One of 25 Children of a Bookseller!

Close Friend of Michel de Montaigne

"All religions have this in common, that they are an outrage to common sense, for they are pieced together out of a variety of elements, some of which seem so unworthy, sordid and at odds with man's reason, that any strong and vigorous intelligence laughs at them"

G K Chesterton

1874-1936 aged 89

Born in Kensington, London

Writer, Philosopher, Poet, Journalist

Lecturer and Art Critic

"The test of a good religion
is whether you can joke about it"

"From time to time, as we all know,
a sect appears in our midst, announcing
that the world will very soon come to an end.
Generally, by some slight confusion
or miscalculation,
it is the sect that
comes to an end"

Noam Chomsky

Born 1928 in Philadelphia
Pennsylvania. Writer, Philosopher
Poet, Journalist, Activist, Lecturer
Linguist, Cognitive Scientist
Art Critic and MIT Professor

"I'm a child of the Enlightenment.
I think irrational belief
is a dangerous thing.
The Bible is one of the most
genocidal books in history.
Three-quarters of the American
population
believe in religious miracles.
The numbers who believe in the devil, in
resurrection, God does this and that...astonishing.
These are numbers that you have nowhere
in the industrial world"

Sir Arthur C Clarke

1917-2008 aged 91

Born in Somerset, England

Science Fiction Writer

Inventor of Satellites and Futurist

"I don't believe in God,

but I'm very interested in her.

One of the great tragedies is that

morality has been hijacked by religion.

Isn't killing people in the name of God

a pretty good definition of insanity?

I would defend the liberty of consenting

adult creationists to practice whatever

intellectual perversions they like,

in the privacy of their own homes;

but it is also necessary to protect the

young and innocent. By the year 3000

all religions will be banned as evil"

Jeremy Clarkson

Born 1960 in Doncaster, Yorkshire

British TV Personality , Writer,

Car Connoisseur and Journalist

"I believe we are born with a moral
compass and we don't need it reset every
Sunday morning by some weird-beard
Communist in a dress. I am completely
unreligious, but it doesn't stop me
trying to be kind to others. If religion
were abolished, it would be a much
much better world"

Bill Clinton

Born 1946 in Hope, Arkansas

42nd President of the United States

Writer and Activist

"Politics is not religion
and we should govern on the basis of
evidence,
not theology.
We have the most religious freedom
of any country in the world, including
the freedom not to believe"

George Clooney

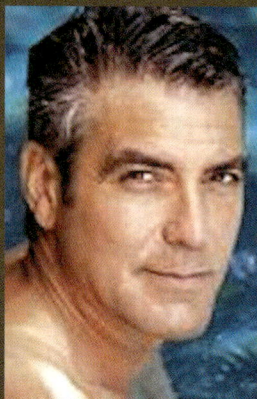

Born 1961 in Lexington, Kentucky
Film and TV Star, Film Director
and Producer and Screenwriter.
Raised Strict Roman Catholic

"I don't believe in
heaven and hell.
I don't know if I believe in God.
All I know is that as an individual,
I won't allow this life, the only thing
I know to exist, to be wasted"

Steven Colbert

Born 1964 in Washington, DC
Writer, Political Satirist
Comedian and TV Host
11th Child of an
Irish Catholic Family

"I believe that everyone has the right to
their own religion, be you Hindu, Jew or
Muslim. I believe there are infinite paths to
accepting Jesus Christ as
your personal Savior!
Remember, Jesus would rather
constantly shame gays
than let orphans have a family"

Samuel Taylor Coleridge

1772-1834 aged 62

Born in Ottery St Mary, Devonshire

English Poet, Critic and Philosopher

"He who begins by loving Christianity better than the Truth, will proceed by loving his own Sect or Church better than Christianity, and end in loving himself better than all. Clergymen who publish pious frauds in the interest of the church are the orthodox liars of God.

Not one man in a thousand has either the strength of mind or goodness of heart to be an atheist. People are free in proportion as they form their own opinions"

Confucius

551 BC-479 BC aged 72

Born in Qufu, China

Chinese Philosopher and Thinker

"The object
of the superior man
is _truth_"

Billy Connolly

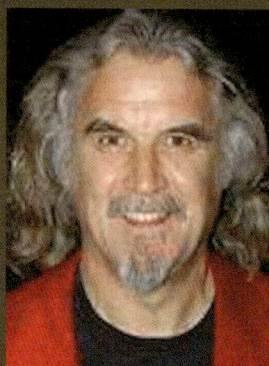

Born 1942 in Glasgow, Scotland

Scottish Comedian,

Musician, Presenter

and Actor

"It seems to me that Islam and
Christianity and Judaism
all have the same god,
and he's telling them all
different things"

Joseph Conrad

1857-1924 aged 67

Born in Berdichev, Ukraine

One of the Greatest English Novelists

He travelled the world while writing

"Outcast of the Islands" "Lord Jim"

"Heart of Darkness"

"Faith is a myth
and beliefs shift like the mist.
Christianity has lent itself with amazing
facility, to cruel distortion, and has brought
an infinity of anguish to innumerable
souls on this earth"

Calvin Coolidge

1872-1933 aged 61

Born in Plymouth Notch, Vermont

30th President of the United States

1923 to 1929

The Only President

Born on the Fourth of July

"We cannot permit any inquisition
either within or without the law
or apply any religious test to the
holding of office.
The mind of America must be free"

Charles Edward Coughlin

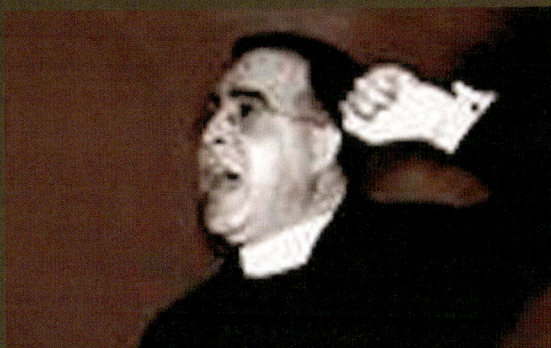

1891-1979 aged 88

Born in Hamilton, Ontario, Canada

Very Controversial Catholic Priest.

In the Nineteen Thirties, 30 million

Americans Listened to His Sunday

Religious Broadcasts Each Week.

"When we get through with the Jews in America, they'll think the treatment they received in Germany was nothing"

Ann Coulter

Born 1961 in New York City
Lawyer, Writer, Columnist, Speaker,
Right Wing Political Commentator
Author and Radio and TV Personality

"I'm a Christian first
and a mean-spirited,
bigoted conservative second.
We should invade their countries,
kill their leaders and convert them to
Christianity.
God gave us the earth.
We have dominion over the plants,
the animals, the trees.
God said 'Earth is yours.
Take it. Rape it. It's yours'"

Sir Noël Coward

1899-1973 aged 74

Born in Teddington, London

English Actor, Playwright

Composer, Singer, Director

"Do I believe in God?

Well yes, I suppose in a sort of a way;

It's really terribly hard to say.

But whether you think me odd or not,

I can't decide if it's God or not.

I look at the changing sea and sky,

I gaze at immensities of blue

and say to myself It can't be true...

that somewhere up there

in that abstract sphere

are all the people who once were here...

attired in white and shapeless gowns,

sitting on clouds like eiderdowns,

plucking on harps and twanging on lutes,

with cherubim in their birthday suits"

Michael Crichton

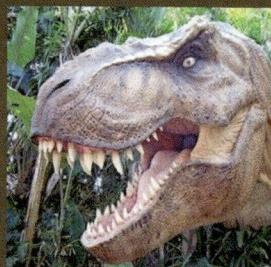

1942-2008 aged 66

Born in Chicago, Illinois

Author, Producer, Director

Screenwriter, Science Fiction Writer

Most Famous for "Jurassic Park"

He Has Sold Over 150 Million Books!

Harvard Trained Physician

"Organized religion is a business and nothing else..
also tells you what to think, and I believe the only
way to know about God is to find out on your own.
What someone else tells you is of very little use...
I believe that we are all God, and God is all of us.
But this means that you can find out everything
you need to know by yourself,
by what you see and what you feel.
Nobody knows more than you do—
even though you're just
in the fifth grade"

Francis Crick

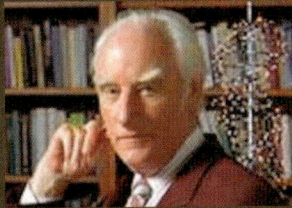

1916-2004 aged 88

Born Near Northampton, England

Molecular Biologist, Biophysicist

Neuroscientist and Co-Discoverer of

the Structure of the DNA Molecule

in 1953 and was Awarded the Nobel Prize

"What could be more foolish than to base one's entire
view of life on ideas that, however plausible at the time,
now appear to be erroneous? And what would be more
important than to find our true place in the universe by
removing one by one, these unfortunate vestiges of
earlier beliefs? If revealed religions have revealed
anything, it is that they are usually wrong.
People believe things that are scientifically false!
If someone tells me that the earth
is less than 10,000 years old,
in my opinion they should
see a psychiatrist!"

Walter Cronkite

1916-2009 aged 93

Born in St Joseph, Missouri

Broadcast Journalist

CBS TV Anchor for 19 Years

From 1962 to 1981

"We know that no one should tell
a woman she has to bear an
unwanted child and we know
that religious beliefs cannot
define patriotism"

Aleister Crowley

1875-1947 aged 72

Born in Leamington Spa, Warwickshire

British Poet, Mystic, Mountaineer

Magician and Occultist

"If one was to take the bible seriously
one would go mad. But to take the bible
seriously, one must be mad already.
The sin which is unpardonable
is knowingly and willfully
to reject the truth,
to fear knowledge,
lest that knowledge
pander not to thy prejudices"

Alan Cumming

Born 1965 in Aberfeldy, Scotland

Stage, Film and TV Actor

in England and America

Director, Producer and Atheist

"I began to realize in church,

that my being part of it

was only

condoning and validating

lots of things I disapprove of

...oppression, guilt and shame"

Marie Curie

1867-1934 aged 67

Born in Warsaw, Poland

Educated and worked at the

Sorbonne in Paris

First Woman Scientist

First Woman to Win a Nobel Prize

First person to Win Two Nobel Prizes

She was the Mother of Modern Physics

She Discovered and Isolated

Radium and Radiation

She was a Pioneer in Radioactivity

She was Brought Up Catholic

But gave Up Catholicism

And Became an Atheist

Dalai Lama

Born 1935 in Takser, Tibet

14th Dalai Lama,

Buddhist Leader

"Be kind whenever possible.

It is always possible.

My religion is very simple.

My religion is kindness.

The purpose of our lives is to be happy.

The roots of all goodness lie in the soil of

appreciation of goodness.

We can live without religion,

but we cannot survive without human

affection. Where ignorance is our master

there is no possibility of real peace"

Clarence Darrow

1857-1938 aged 81

Born in Kinsman, Ohio

One of America's Most Famous Defense Lawyers

Renowned for his Defense in the "Monkey Trial"

In Tennessee in 1925 When John Scopes was

Barred from Teaching Evolution

"In spite of the yearnings of men, no one can

produce a single fact or reason to support the

belief in God and in personal immortality.

I believe that religion is the belief in future life

and in God. I don't believe in either.

I don't believe in God

as I don't believe in Mother Goose

Some of you say religion makes people happy.

So does laughing gas, so does whiskey.

Charles Darwin

1809-1882 aged 73

Born in Shrewsbury, Shropshire
English Naturalist and Writer

"The mystery of the beginning of all things
is insoluble by us, and I for one must
be content to remain an agnostic.
I cannot persuade myself that a beneficent
and omnipotent God would have
designedly created..
that a cat should play with a mouse.
I can hardly see how anyone ought to wish
Christianity to be true; that men who do not
believe, and this would include my Father,
Brother and almost all my best friends,
will be everlastingly punished.
And that is a damnable doctrine"

Larry David

Born 1947 in Brooklyn, New York.

Actor, Comedian, Writer and Producer

Co-Creator of TV's "Seinfeld"

Creator and Star of TV's

"Curb Your Enthusiasm"

"Religion <u>should</u> be made fun of...it's quite ridiculous, isn't it! If <u>I</u> believed all that stuff, I'd keep it to myself, lest people would think I was out of my mind!"

Richard Dawkins

Born 1941 in Nairobi, Kenya

British Ethnologist and

Evolutionary Biologist

Leading Atheist and Critic of

Creationism and Intelligent Design

"We are all atheists about the gods that other societies have believed in. Some of us just go one god further. When you understand why you dismiss all the other gods, you will understand why I dismiss yours. All religious beliefs seem weird to people not brought up in them. Faith is the great cop-out, the excuse to evade the need to think and evaluate evidence. Faith is belief in spite of, even perhaps because of, the lack of evidence. Its independence from evidence is its pride and joy. I am against religion because it teaches us to be satisfied with not understanding the world and I am very hostile to religion because it is enormously dominant, especially in American life"

Richard Dawkins...continued

"It's a remarkable coincidence that almost everyone has the same religion as their parents and it always just so happens they're the right religion. The convictions you so passionately believe, would have been completely different and largely contradictory, if you had been born in a different place.

<u>Scientific</u> beliefs are supported by <u>evidence</u>, and they get results. Myths and faiths are not and do not. Faith is capable of driving people to such dangerous folly, that faith seems to me to qualify as a kind of mental illness...and I don't buy the argument that, well, it's harmless. I think it is harmful, partly because I care passionately about what's true.

The God of the Old Testament is arguably the most unpleasant character in all fiction; jealous and proud of it; a petty, unjust, unforgiving control-freak; a vindictive, bloodthirsty ethnic cleanser; a misogynistic, homophobic, racist, infanticidal, genocidal, filicidal, pestilential, megalomaniacal, sadomasochistic, capriciously malevolent bully"

Tom DeLay

Born 1947 in Laredo, Texas

Born-Again Christian

Former Republican

House Majority Leader, He Resigned

Because of Money Laundering

Charges, Convicted and Sentenced

to 3 Years in Prison.

"God is using me, all the time,
everywhere, to stand up for a
biblical worldview in everything
that I do and everywhere I am.
He is training me"

Daniel Dennett

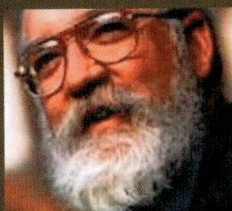

Born 1942 in Boston, Massachusetts
Philosopher, Cognitive Scientist, Atheist
One of the "Four Horsemen" of the New Atheism
With Richard Dawkins, Christopher Hitchens,
and Sam Harris

"The idea that God is a worthy recipient of
our gratitude for the blessings of life, but
should not be held accountable for the
disasters, is a transparently disingenuous
innovation of the theologians. You don't
have to be religious to be crazy, but it helps.
Indeed, if you are religious, you don't have to
be certifiably crazy, to do massively crazy
things. There are no forces more dangerous
than the fanaticisms of fundamentalism"

Alan Dershowitz

Born 1938 in Brooklyn, New York

Distinguished American Lawyer

Professor at Harvard Law School since 1967

"Religion is always having to say you're
sorry for misunderstanding God's will.
I don't know whether God exists.
If there is a God who is threatening me
with damnation because I don't believe in
Him, so be it, a tyrannical God who would
damn me, that because of the
intelligence He gave me, I have come to a
conclusion doubting his existence"

Charles Dickens

1812-1870 aged 58

Born in Portsmouth, Hampshire

The Most Popular English Novelist

of the Victorian Era

Nothing

more surely aroused his suspicions

about a person's religious faith,

than a public profession of it.

He had a life-long aversion to

evangelism.

Marlene Dietrich

1901-1992 aged 91

Born in Berlin, Germany

German/American Film

and Stage Star and Singer

"If there is

a supreme being,

he's crazy.

I've given up any belief in God.

As Goethe said,

If God created this world,

then he should review his plan"

Phyllis Diller

1915-2012 aged 95

American Actress and Comedienne

One of the Pioneers of Stand-Up Comedy

She once mentioned in passing

that she's an atheist,

although she was high

at the time...

40,000 feet high!

"Religion is such a medieval idea.

don't get me started...

it's all about the money!"

Walt Disney

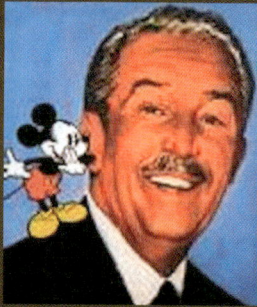

1901-1966 aged 65

Born in Chicago, Illinois

Film Producer, Director, Screenwriter

Animator, Entrepreneur

International Icon

As an adult, Disney was not religious,
he did not attend church
and did not teach his children
to follow any specific denomination.

Benjamin Disraeli

1804-1881 aged 77

Born in London

Britain's Victorian Era

Prime Minister

First and Only Jewish PM

Was Prime Minister Twice

Once in 1868 and Again From

1874 to 1880

Novelist and Brilliant Debater

"Where knowledge ends
religion begins"

Gregory Dix

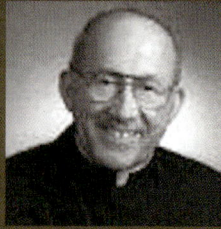

1901-1952 aged 51

Born in Woolwich, Kent

English Benedictine Monk

Influential Controversialist

"It is no accident that the symbol

of a Bishop is a Crook

and the Sign of an Archbishop

is a Double-Cross"

Amanda Donahoe

Born 1962 in London

English Stage, Screen and TV Star

Has Made Many Films in Hollywood

"I can't embrace a male god
who has persecuted female
sexuality throughout the ages.
And that persecution
still goes on today
all over the world"

Frederick Douglass

1818-1895 aged 77

Born a slave in Maryland

Escaped from Slavery to become a Writer, Orator, Social Reformer, Statesman and a Leader of the Abolition of Slavery Movement. He Drew Huge Crowds on a Two Year Lecture Tour of England and Ireland and in America too.

"The Church of this country is not only indifferent to the wrongs of the slave, it actually takes sides with the oppressors...For my part, I would say, welcome infidelity! Welcome atheism! Welcome anything! In preference to the gospel, as preached by those Divines! They convert the very name of religion into an engine of tyranny, and barbarous cruelty, and serve to confirm more infidels, in this age, than all the infidel writings of Thomas Paine, Voltaire, and Bolingbroke put together, have done!"

Margaret Downey

Born 1950 in Baton Rouge,

Louisiana

Former President of the

Atheist Alliance International

"I was quite content discussing religion only when I was asked, but when our son was ousted from the Boys Scouts of America, for being from an atheist family, it made me so angry I began to speak out about the injustice"

THERE ARE OVER FIVE MILLION ATHEISTS IN THE US AND WITH AGNOSTICS AND NON-RELIGIOUS IT'S MORE LIKE TWENTY MILLION AMERICANS

Richard Dreyfuss

Born 1947 in Brooklyn, New York

Award Winning Actor

Films TV and Stage

"We in America are the

actualization of the

enlightenment,

where reason and logic and

scientific deduction and

<u>intelligence</u>

are considered better than

Faith, Hope and Zealotry"

David Duchovny

Born 1960 in New York City

Award Winning Actor

In Films and TV

"People don't want to get in bed
with science because it's cold.

They prefer

Religion, Myth, Drama"

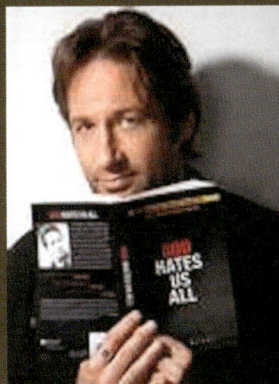

Sir Arthur Eddington

1882-1944 aged 62

Born in Kendal, Cumbria,

British Astrophysicist.

In 1919, He Explained Einstein's

Theory of General Relativity

to the English Speaking World

"Not only is the universe

stranger that we imagine,

it is stranger than we _can_ imagine"

"There once was a brainy baboon

Who always breathed down a bassoon

For he said "It appears

That in billions of years

I shall certainly hit on a tune"

Thomas Edison

1847-1931 aged 84

Born in Milan, Ohio

American Inventor,

Scientist and Businessman

"I have never seen the slightest proof
of heaven and hell. All this talk of
existence beyond the grave is wrong.
It is born of our tenacity of life, our
desire to go on living, our dread of
coming to an end.
Religion is a damned fake!
Religion is all bunk!
We don't know one millionth
of one percent about anything!"

Jonathan Edwards

Born 1966 in London

Olympic, Commonwealth, European
and World champion Long Jumper
In 2007 He Became an Atheist

"I feel slightly embarrassed about how
devoutly Christian I once was.
I think I was quite narrow-minded
and fundamental in my views.
I believed that what I believed was true.
It's not where I am now.
Athletes tend to believe that god will give
them a win. That's nonsense"

Barbara Ehrenreich

Born 1941 in Butte, Montana
American Feminist, Sociologist
and Political Activist

"Frankly I adore your catchy slogan
"Adoption, Not Abortion" although no one
has been able to figure out, even with expert
counseling, how to use adoption as a method
of birth control or at what time of the month
it is most effective. Roman Catholicism:
a hundred million people bowing down
before an elderly, flesh-hating celibate.
The Republican Party: a few million
gun-toting, Armageddon-ready Baptists.
Jesus: a wine-guzzling vagrant.
and precocious socialist"

Albert Einstein

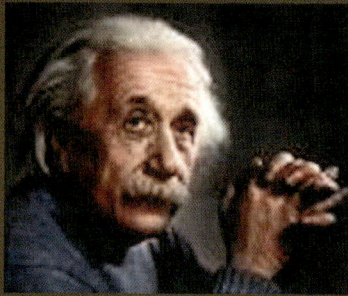

1879-1955 aged 76

Born in Ulm, Germany

Theoretical Physicist

"I came to a deep religiosity, which came to
an abrupt end age 12. I do not believe in a
personal God. If people are good only because
they fear punishment and hope of reward
then we are a sorry lot indeed.
The idea of a personal God is a childlike one.
From the viewpoint of a Jesuit priest,
I am, of course, and have always been
an atheist, a deeply religious non-believer.
Does religion promote peace?
It has not done so up to now"

Dwight Eisenhower

1890-1969 aged 79

Born in Denison, Texas

Five Star General in the

United States Army

Supreme Commander Allied Forces

in World War Two

34th President of the United States, 1953-1961

"From this day forward,
the millions of our school children will
daily proclaim in every city, village
and rural schoolhouse the dedication of
our Nation and our people to the
Almighty"

Havelock Ellis

1859-1939 aged 80

Born in Croydon, Surrey

English Physician, Psychologist

Writer and Social Reformer

Who Studied Human Sexuality

"There is a very intimate connection between hypnotic phenomena and religion"

Ralph Waldo Emerson

1803-1882 aged 79

Born in Boston, Massachusetts

Philosopher, Lecturer,

Essayist and Poet

"If I should go out of church

whenever I hear a false sentiment,

I should never stay there five minutes.

As men's prayers are a disease of the will,

so are their creeds a disease of the intellect.

The religion of one age, is the literary

entertainment of the next"

Lou Engle

Born in Kansas City, Missouri
American Evangelical Leader
of the Christian Right
He Draws Crowds of Over 100,000 Followers
to His 12 Hour Prayer Rallies
In May 2010, He Went to Uganda and set in
motion the Persecution and Deaths of
Ugandan Gays and Lesbians.
And in 2008 When California Legalized
Same-Sex Marriages, He Said:
"What happened will release a spirit
more demonic than Islam, a spirit
of lawlessness and anarchy. And a
sexual insanity will be unleashed"

Epicurus

341 BC-270 BC aged 71

Born on the Island of Samos

Greek Philosopher

"Is God

willing to prevent evil,

but not able?

Then he is not omnipotent.

Is he able, but not willing?

Then he is malevolent.

Is he both able and willing?

Then whence cometh evil?

Is he neither able nor willing?

Then why call him God?

Reverend Jerry Falwell

1933-2007 aged 74

Born in Lynchburg, Virginia

Christian Evangelical Fundamentalist

Southern Baptist Pastor & Televangelist

"Good Christians, like slaves and soldiers, ask no questions. Grown men should not be having sex with prostitutes, unless they are married to them. AIDS is not just God's punishment for homosexuals; it is God's punishment for the society that tolerates homosexuals. Gays, lesbians and feminists helped the terrorist attacks on 9/11 happen. I feel that most ministers who claim they've heard God's voice, are eating too much pizza before they go to bed at night, and it's really an intestinal disorder, not a revelation. If you're not a born-again Christian, you're a failure as a human being. The idea that religion and politics don't mix was invented by the devil, to keep Christians from running their own country .Oh, and Archbishop Tutu is a phony"

Christopher Hitchens said:

"If you gave Falwell an enema,
he could be buried in a matchbox"

Jules Feiffer

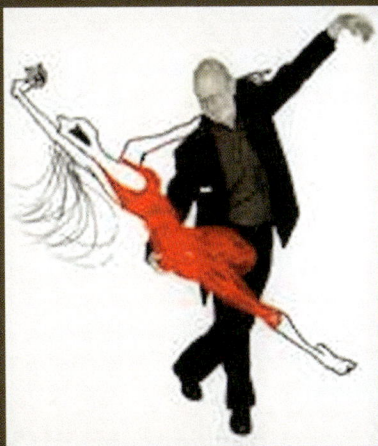

Born 1929 in The Bronx, New York

Pulitzer Prize Winning

American Cartoonist

He Has Created Over 35 Books

Some Plays and a Screenplay

"Christ died for our sins.
Dare we make his martyrdom
meaningless, by not
committing them?"

Federico Fellini

1920-1993 aged 73

Born in Rimini, Italy

Italian Filmmaker

Who Blended Fantasy and Baroque Images

and was one of the

Most Influential Directors

"Like many people, I have no religion.
Churches don't want free men who can
think for themselves. I am just sitting
in a small boat, drifting with the tide. I
think there is dignity in this, just to go on
working. We stand naked, defenseless and
more alone than at any time in history"

Geraldine Ferraro

1935-2011 aged 76

Born in Newburgh, New York

American Attorney

Democratic Politician

First Female Vice Presidential

Candidate with Walter Mondale

in his Run for President in 1984

"Personal religious convictions
have no place in political
campaigns"

Francisco Ferrer

1859-1909 aged 50
Born near Barcelona, Spain
Spanish Catalan Free Thinker
and Crusader Against Religion.
The Last European Citizen
Executed for Heresy.
"When the masses become better
informed about science, they will
feel less need for help from
Supernatural Higher Forces"

Richard Feynman

1918-1988 aged 70

Born in Queens, New York.

Nobel Prize-winning Caltech Physicist and
Raconteur, known for his work in quantum
mechanics and quantum electrodynamics

"If 50 million people believe a foolish thing,
it is still a foolish thing.

God is always invented to explain those things that
you do not understand. During the Middle Ages there
were all kinds of crazy ideas, such as that a piece of
rhinoceros horn would make you hornier.

Then a method was discovered for separating the
ideas, which was to try one to see if it worked,
and if it didn't work, to eliminate it.

This method became organized, of course, into
SCIENCE"

W C Fields

1880~1946 aged 66

Born in Darby, Pennsylvania

"To me, these biblical stories are just so many fish stories, not just Jonah and the Whale...I need indisputable proof of anything I'm asked to believe. More people are driven insane through religious hysteria, than by drinking alcohol. If ever I found a church that didn't believe in knocking all the other religions, I might consider joining it. I think of church often, not because of religion, but because my ass is still sore from that hard, un-upholstered pew. Prayer may bring solace to the sap, the bigot, the ignorant, the aboriginal, and the lazy, but really it's the same as asking Santa to bring you something for Christmas. You can fool some of the people some of the time, and that's enough to make a decent living. Start every day with a smile, get it over with. Thou shalt not take the Lord's name in vain, unless you've used up all the other four-letter words. I scanned the Bible once, searching for some movie plots, but found only a pack of lies. Oh, I did look it over on my deathbed, looking for loopholes"

Harvey Fierstein

Born 1952 in Brooklyn, New York

Award Winning Entertainer

Actor, Activist and Playwright

"I'm a Jewish atheist...I pray every day
but I don't believe in God or heaven or hell.
Beware of anyone who says they KNOW.
Trust me, they don't,
or they wouldn't have said they did.
The Catholic Church is the only organization
on record to dispense money from a slush fund set
up solely for the paying off of abused children's
families. So always remember,
you cannot judge a man by his collar"

Carrie Fisher

Born 1956 in Beverly Hills California

Actress, Writer

and Screenwriter

Daughter of Eddie Fisher

and Debbie Reynolds.

Author of "Wishful Drinking"

"Karl Marx said

"Religion is the opiate of the masses"...

I did masses of opiates religiously"

"Sometimes you can only find Heaven

by slowly backing away from Hell"

F Scott Fitzgerald

1896-1940 aged 44

Born in St Paul, Minnesota

Great American Writer

"The Great Gatsby" etc

"I know myself
but that is all"

"Either you think...
or else others have to think for you
and take away your power.
You can take your choice between
God and Sex.
If you choose both, you're a hypocrite;
If neither, you get nothing"

Brian Flemming

Born in the San Fernando Valley, California
but like Christ, we don't know when.
Filmmaker and Screenwriter,
Made "The God Who Wasn't There"
"I'm a former Christian...but I gradually realized
I was an atheist. I thought that Fundamentalist
Christianity was wrong, but that Christianity was
probably right. Then, the more I thought about it,
the more I deduced my way to atheism. You see, to
me, an atheist is someone who has looked really
hard at the argument for God, and found it to be
extremely lacking. I consider the chance that God
exists to be vanishingly small, to the point where
it's pointless to be thinking about it any further.
The problem is that we let religious people say
stunningly false things, and we consider it rude
to question those beliefs. I'm not tolerant of
suspending REASON"

Larry Flynt

Born 1942 in Lakeville, Kentucky

American Publisher of Hustler Magazine

An assassination attempt in 1978 left him

paralyzed from the waist down.

That ended his one year conversion to Christianity.

In 1988, the Supreme Court Ruled Against Jerry

Falwell in his lawsuit against Flynt over a

satirical item in Hustler, suggesting that Falwell's

first sexual experience was with his mother!

"I have left my religious conversion behind, and

settled into..atheism. I have come to think that

religion has caused more harm than any other idea

since the beginning of time.

The Jerry Falwells of this world are living proof of

the hypocrisy that permeates organized religion

in America and around the world"

Peter Fonda

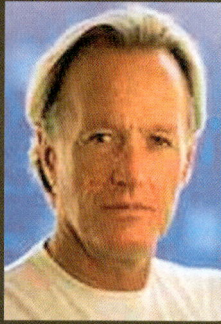

Born 1940 in New York City
Film Star Son of Henry Fonda
and Brother of Jane Fonda
"I'm a Naturalist. We believe that man
is doomed by his myths, that there can be
no peace on Earth until man rids himself
of all belief in the supernatural. I've
never thought there was another world
better than this one. To doubt is not
blasphemy. When you say blasphemy,
you mean... don't dare disagree,
don't think, don't doubt"

Harrison Ford

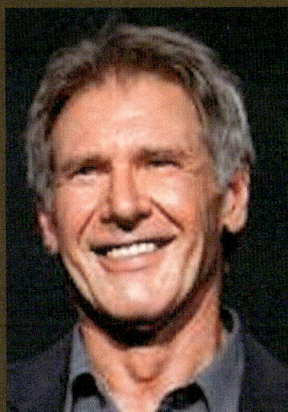

Born 1942 in Chicago, Illinois

One of the Leading Movie Stars

"Star Wars" and "Indiana Jones" etc

"If you have trouble with the word God,
Take whatever is central, or meaningful
in your life, and call that God"
An Agnostic,
when asked in what religion
he was raised, he replied
"Democrat!"

E M Forster

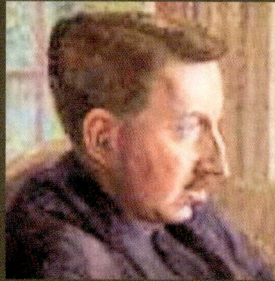

1879-1970 aged 91

Born in London

Novelist, Humanist and Homosexual

"Passage to India" "Maurice" etc

"Faith, to my mind, is a stiffening process,
a sort of mental starch, which ought to be
applied as sparingly as possible...
I do not believe in it for its
own sake at all. Sudden conversion
is particularly attractive to the
half-baked mind. There lies at
the back of every creed something
terrible and hard. I'm a holy man,
minus the holy"

Jody Foster

Born 1962 in Los Angeles
California
Film Star Since Childhood,
Film Director and Producer

"How could you ask me to
believe in God
when there's absolutely
no evidence that I can see"

John Fowles

1926-2005 aged 79

Born in Leigh-on-Sea, Essex

English Novelist, Essayist

and Poet

"Being an atheist
is a matter
not of moral choice,
but of human obligation"

Al Franken

Born 1951 in New York City

United States Senator for Minnesota

Graduated cum laude From Harvard

Comedian and Political Satirist

Writer and Actor for 15 Years on
"Saturday Night Live"

Author of Five #1 Best Sellers

"The religious right
sometimes forget we don't live in a theocracy.
They can express their opinion, but to expect other
people to alter their behavior to say for example,
that homosexuality is immoral because it says so in
the Bible...I mean it also says you can't eat pork.
I don't see a lot of orthodox Jews saying people who eat
pork shouldn't be allowed to get insurance benefits.
I mean, there's stuff in the Bible about how
to sell your daughter"

Benjamin Franklin

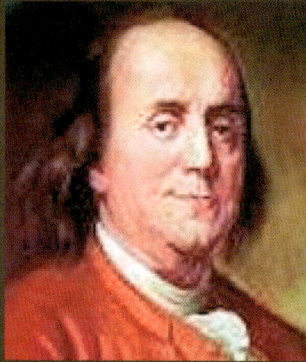

1706-1790 aged 84

Born in Boston, Massachusetts

Writer, Scientist, Printer, Polymath

Author, Revolutionary and

One of the Founding Fathers

"Religion I found to be without any tendency to inspire, promote, or confirm morality, serves principally to divide us and make us unfriendly one to another. I have found Christian dogma unintelligible. Early in life I absented myself from Christian assemblies. The way to see by faith, is to shut the eye of reason. Lighthouses are more helpful than churches. Every sect supposes itself in possession of all truth"

Frederick the Great

1740-1786 aged 46

Born in Berlin

King of Prussia

close Friend of Voltaire

"Theologians are all alike, of whatever
religion or country they may be;
their aim is always to wield despotic
authority over men's consciences;
they therefore persecute all of us who have
the temerity to tell the truth.
Of all plagues with which mankind is cursed
ecclesiastical tyrannies are worst"

Morgan Freeman

Born 1937 in Memphis,

Tennessee

African/American

Film Star

and Director

He tends to see traditional religion

as a meaningless ritual with little

to offer, and is eager to experiment

with other, alternative paths.

Sigmund Freud

1856-1939 aged 83

Born in Freiburg, Austria

Founder of Psychoanalysis

"Religion is the process of unconscious wish
fulfillment, and is comparable to a childhood
neurosis. Religion is an illusion and it derives its
strength from the fact that it falls in
with our instinctual desires. No one who shares
a delusion, ever recognizes it as such.
Most people do not want freedom, because
freedom involves responsibility, and most people
are frightened of responsibility. Neither in my
private life, nor in my writings, have I ever
made a secret of being an out-and-out
unbeliever"

Erich Fromm

1900-1980 aged 80

Born in Frankfurt-am-Main,
German/American
Psychoanalyst and Philosopher

"If faith cannot be reconciled with
rational thinking, it has to be
eliminated as an anachronistic
remnant of earlier stages of culture
and replaced by science dealing with
facts and theories which are
intelligible and can be validated"

Stephen Fry

Born 1957 in Hampstead, London

Writer, Actor, Comedian, Director

"If ignorance is bliss, why aren't there more happy people in the world? I am a lover of truth, a worshiper of freedom, and a celebrant at the altar of language and purity and tolerance. That is my religion, and I am deeply offended by a thousand different blasphemies against it, when truth, honesty, compassion and decency are assaulted by fatuous bishops, pompous priests, politicians and prelates, sanctimonious censors, self-appointed moralists and busy-bodies. On the subject of texts, like a Bible or a Qur'an..the greatness of our culture, for all its faults, is that we have the Greek ideal of discovering the <u>truth</u>, by empirical experiment and the experience of generations of ancestors who have contributed to our sum knowledge of the way the world works"

R Buckminster Fuller

1895-1983 aged 88

Born in Milton, Massachusetts

American Inventor, Engineer

Architect, Designer, Philosopher

Author and Futurist

Designer of the Geodesic Dome

Published Over 30 Books

"Sometimes I think we're alone.

Sometimes I think we're not.

In either case

the thought is quite staggering"

Richard Furman

1755-1825 aged 70

Born in Esopus, New York

Raised in Charleston, South Carolina

Influential Baptist Leader

"The right of holding slaves is clearly established in the Holy Scriptures. Had the holding of slaves been a moral evil, it cannot be that the inspired Apostles would have tolerated it in the Christian Church. In proving it justifiable by Scriptural authority (Luke 12:47) * its morality is also proved; for the Divine Law never sanctions immoral actions"

*THE SLAVE WHO KNEW HIS MASTER'S WILL BUT DID NOT GET READY OR ACT ACCORDING TO HIS WILL, WILL RECEIVE A SEVERE BEATING

Yuri Gagarin

1934-1968 aged 34

Born in Klushino, Russia

Soviet Pilot and Cosmonaut

First Person Ever in Space

He Orbited the Earth in 1961

a Total of 24,800 Miles

Weightless for 89 Minutes

"I don't see any

god

up here"

Galileo Galilei

1564-1642 aged 78

Born in Pisa, Italy

Astronomer, Physicist,

Mathematician and Philosopher

When the Catholic Church Pressured Him to

Support Their Belief That the Sun Revolved

Around the Earth

"You command astronomers to not see what they

do see, and not to understand what they do

understand, and to find what they do not discover. I

do not feel obliged to believe that the same God who

has endowed us with sense, reason and intellect,

wished us to forego their use"

Galileo and the Pope Were Friends and the Pope

Told Him 'You're right, I agree with you, but I

can't agree with you publicly, it would cause too

much upheaval in the Catholic church"

So Galileo suffered the Inquisition and House Arrest

Indira Gandhi

1917-1984 aged 67

Born in Allahabad, India

India's 3rd Prime Minister

For Three consecutive Terms

1966 to 1977 and a 4th Term

From 1980 Until Her Assassination.

Daughter of India's

1st Prime Minister, Nehru.

"There exists no politician in India,
daring enough to attempt to explain to
the masses, that cows can be eaten"

Mahatma Gandhi

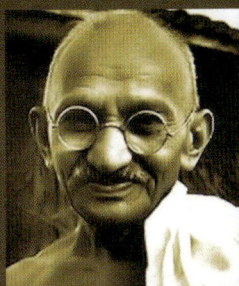

1869-1948 aged 79

Born in Porbandar, India

Pioneer of India's

Independence from Britain

Assassinated by a Hindu Nationalist

"The most cruel crimes throughout history
have been committed under the cover of
religion. There is no god higher than truth.
I love your Christ. It's just that so many
Christians are so unlike your Christ.
Yes, I'm a Hindu. I am also a Christian,
a Muslim, a Buddhist and a Jew.
You think I'm superstitious?
I'm a super-atheist"

William M Gaines

1922-1992 aged 70

Born in Brooklyn, New York

Founder & Publisher of "MAD" Magazine

Hugely Popular Since 1952

Here's His Cover Boy, Alfred E Nueman

"On my honor as an atheist...

You're a group of Christian-based

organizations with several million dollars

to spend.

Do you: Feed the hungry?

Clothe the poor? Don't be so naïve!

You blow the million on a series of slickly-worded,

logic-bending ads espousing a widely-discredited

theory that one can be "cured" of homosexuality

through counseling and prayer"

PRAY AWAY THE GAY!

Bill Gates

Born 1955 in Seattle, Washington

American Billionaire

Business Magnate

Philanthropist and Author

Chairman of Microsoft

One of the World's Wealthiest Men

"Just in terms of allocation of
resources, religion is not very efficient.
There's a lot more I could be doing on a
Sunday morning"

Sir Bob Geldof

Born 1951 in Dun Laoghaire

(Pronounced Dun Leary!)

Ireland

Irish Rock Musician

Singer, Songwriter, Author

and Humanitarian

Activist Against Poverty in Africa

"Am I a saint or a sinner?

Being an atheist,

I can't be either"

Ricky Gervais

Born 1961 in Reading, Berkshire

British Comedian, Film & TV Actor

Director, Producer, Musician & Writer

"I used to be very religious, I loved Jesus. But one afternoon when I was 8, I stopped and thought about it, and I realized that religion is all based on a big bunch of lies"

André Gide

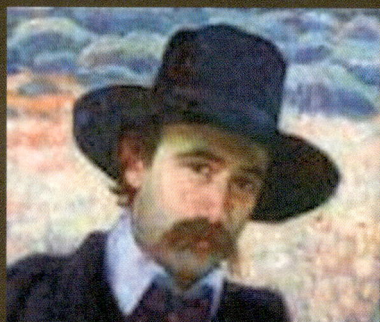

1869-1951 aged 82

Born in Paris

French Author

Nobel Prize Winner in 1947

for Literature

"Believe those who seek

the truth,

doubt those who find it,

doubt all,

but do not doubt yourself"

Julia Gillard

Born 1961 in Barry, Wales
In 1966 Moved to
Adelaide, Australia
She Became Australia's
Prime Minister in 2010
"I have no intention
of pretending
I believe in God to attract
religious voters"

Newt Gingrich

Born 1943 in Harrisburg, Pennsylvania
Born again in 1960. Married 3 Times.
Republican Politician Former Speaker of the
House of Representatives, Resigned in 1998
Having denounced Clinton for his Affair, While
Secretly Having One Himself. Explaining on TV
"I love my country so passionately, I overworked
& did some things that were not appropriate"
He now warns that "The US could become a secular
atheist country dominated by radical Islamists.
A cultural elite are trying to create a secular
America in which God is driven out of public life"
He was running for President in 2012,
but Congressman Al Franken said Newt is the most
unpopular politician in America, "His favorable
rating is only 4 points higher than the Uni Bomber"

Whoopi Goldberg

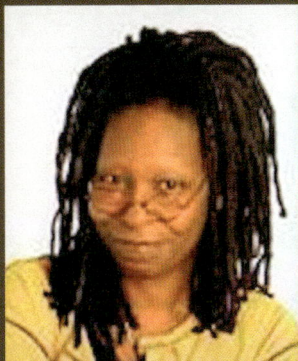

Born 1955 in New York City

Comedian, Film and TV Star

Singer-Songwriter

Talk Show Host

Political Activist

"My family is Jewish, Buddhist,
Baptist and Catholic...
I don't believe in
man-made religions...period.
Religion has done more to bust up
humanity than anything"

Emma Goldman

1869-1951 aged 82

Born in Kovno, Russia

Russian-American Writer

Activist, Anarchist and Atheist

She emigrated to New York in 1885

"Atheism is the eternal Yea to

Life, Purpose and Beauty.

I do not believe in God, because I believe in

Man. Christianity is most admirably

adapted to the training of slaves. There

are some potentates I would kill. They are

Ignorance, Superstition and Bigotry"

Barry Goldwater

1909-1998 aged 89

Born in Phoenix, Arizona

5 Term Moderate Republican Arizona Senator

Ran for President in 1964

"I think every good Christian should kick Jerry Falwell right in the ass! I'm frankly sick and tired of preachers telling me how to be a moral person. Just who do they think they are, that they claim the right to dictate their moral beliefs to me? I will fight them every step of the way if they try to dictate their moral convictions to all Americans in the name of conservatism, demanding their own version of heaven on earth, and let me remind you, they are the very ones who create the most hellish tyranny.

Incidentally, you don't have to be straight to be in the military, you just have to able to shoot straight"

Mikhail Gorbachev

Born 1931 in Stavropol, Russia

Former Soviet President

Mr Gobachev <u>Did</u> Tear Down That Wall

and Initiated Perestroika and Glasnost

and the End of Soviet Communism

"Jesus was the first socialist, the first to seek a better life for mankind"

Nadine Gordimer

Born 1923 in Johannesburg, South Africa

Won the Nobel Prize for Literature, in 1991

"I'm an atheist, but if anyone could ever launch me
into the belief of a religious faith, it would have
been Archbishop Desmond Tutu.
I have no religious faith,
but when I look at that photograph of
Trevor Huddleston, a profoundly religious man,
I see godliness in a way I can understand.
Truth isn't always beauty
...but the hunger for it is"

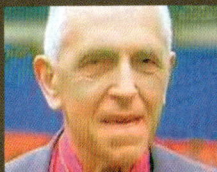

Rev Trevor Huddleston, 1913-1998 aged 85
Author of "Naught For Your Comfort"

Al Gore

Born 1948 in Washington, DC

45th Vice President with

President Bill Clinton

Democratic Nominee for President 2000

He Got More Votes than Bush who was

"appointed" by the Supreme Court.

Has since warned the World about

Global Warming/Climate Change

for Which He Won

the Nobel Peace Prize in 2007

"I affirm my faith when asked, but

with respect..for those who do not

believe in God and who are atheists"

Stephen Jay Gould

1941-2002 aged 61

Born in Queens, New York

Paleontologist, Interpreter of Science ,
Evolutionary Biologist and Agnostic
"The long, sad history of
American anti-intellectualism.
Evolution is one of the best documented,
most compelling and exciting concepts in
all of science. The most important scientific
revolutions include the dethronement of
human arrogance about our centrality in
the cosmos. Human life is the result of a
glorious evolutionary accident"

Rev. Billy Graham

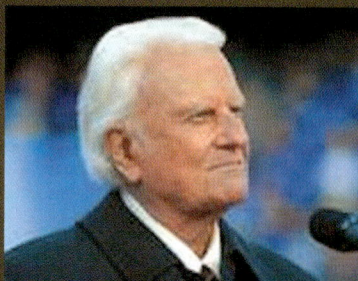

Born 1918 in Charlotte, North Carolina

Southern Baptist Evangelist

"Boring Racist Charlatan

from Charlotte"

According to Christopher Hitchens!

Mentor to 12 Presidents, Since Truman

"I don't want to see religious bigotry in

any form. It would disturb me if there

was a wedding between the religious

fundamentalists and the political

right. The hard right has no interest in

religion except to manipulate it"

Ulysses Grant

1822-1885 aged 63

Born in Point Pleasant, Ohio

18th President of the United States

From 1869 to 1877

Military Commander of the Union Army
in the Civil War 1861 until 1865 When He
Captured Richmond and Ended the War.

"I would like to draw your attention to
an _evil_ that, if allowed to continue, will
probably lead to great trouble. It is the
accumulation of _vast_ amounts of
Untaxed church property"

Ruth Hurmence Green

1915-1981 aged 66

Born in Sumner, Iowa

"Born Again Skeptic" And Writer

"It was reading the Bible
cover to cover that turned me into an atheist.
I'm convinced that children should not be subjected
to the frightfulness of the Christian religion..
if the concept of a father who plots to have his own
son put to death, is presented to children as
beautiful and as worthy of society's admiration,
what types of human behavior can be presented as
reprehensible?
It is possible to pull out justification for imposing
your will on others, simply by calling your will,
God's will"

Kate Greenaway

1846-1901 aged 55

Born in London

English Painter, Writer

And Illustrator of

Children's Books

"It is strange beyond
anything I can think,
to be able to believe any
of the known religions"

Graham Greene

1904-1991 aged 87

Born in Berkhamstead

Hertfordshire

Roman Catholic

English Novelist, Journalist

and Playwright

"Heresy

is only another word for

freedom of thought"

Germaine Greer

Born 1939 in Melbourne,

Australia

Writer, Academic

Journalist and Feminist

"The blind conviction that we have to do something about other people's reproductive behavior, and that we may do it, whether they like it or not, derives from the assumption that the world belongs to us, who have expertly depleted its resources"

Pope Gregory I

540-604 aged 64

Born in Rome, Italy

"Gregory The Great"

Reigned as Pope from 590 to 604

He Had the Patriarch of Constantinople

Burned at the Stake

For Not Following Rome Dogma!

"The bliss of the elect in heaven would not
be perfect unless they were able to look
across the abyss and enjoy the agonies of
their brethren in eternal fire"
NICE!

Pope Gregory VI

1015-1085 aged 70

Born in Tuscany, Italy

Bought the Papacy from his Young

Godson, Pope Benedict IX,

who Abdicated so He Could Marry.

He Reigned as Pope from 1073 to 1085

"From the polluted fountain
of that absurd and erroneous doctrine, or
rather raving, which claims and defends
liberty of conscience for everyone, comes,
in a word, the worst plague of all—
liberty of opinions and free speech"

Kathy Griffin

Born 1960 in Chicago, Illinois

Award Winning Comedienne,

Writer, Entertainer & Activist

"I'm a fallen Catholic!"

She upset Catholics and other Christians

when she won an Emmy Award saying

"A lot of people come up here and thank

Jesus for this award. I want you to know

that no one had less to do with this award

than Jesus!"

Donald Henry Gudehus

Born 1939 in Jersey City, New Jersey
American Astronomer and Composer

"Religion is like cigarettes,
too much of it stunts the growth...
in this case, of the intellect and the emotions.
An effective counter to the endless succession of zealotry
and fanaticism from one generation to the next, with
its ill effect on scientific enquiry, thought, freedom
of expression and behavior, would be to institute
an age of consent for religious indoctrination.
The history of religion can be compared to a layer cake;
a mountain of layers of stale dogma interspersed
with the congealed blood of its victims,
overlaid with a sweetened opiate to make
itself appealing to the gullible"

Che Guevara

1928-1967 aged 39

Born in Rosario, Argentina

Revolutionary, Politician, Physician

Intellectual, Author and Atheist

Lived and Died a Revolutionary

"We cannot be indifferent to what happens
anywhere in the world, for a victory in any
country, is our victory, just as any country's
defeat, is a defeat for all of us"

Che Tshirts are among the first things you see at
Havana Airport. At least Cubans know whom
they are idolizing. In the US, Che's life story
and ambitions seem beside the point.
The man's face is shorthand for
'I'm against the status quo'"

Ken Ham

Born 1951 in Queensland, Australia

Evangelist Who Advocates Literal Interpretation
of the Book of Genesis

As a Young Earth Creationist, He Believes the Entire
Universe was Created 6,000 Years Ago, and That Humans
Co-existed with Dinosaurs! A Huge 27 Million Dollar
Museum to "Prove" it, has been Created in Kentucky!

"If you can't trust the Bible's history,
how can you trust it's morality?"!

Next They Plan a Full Size 150 Million Dollar
Replica of Noah's Ark!

Butch Hancock

Born in Lubbock, Texas

Country Singer

and Musician

"Life in Lubbock, Texas

taught me two things:

One is that God loves you

and you're going to burn in hell.

And the other thing is that sex

is the most awful thing on earth

and you should

save it for someone

you love!"

Tony Hancock

1924-1968 aged 44

Born in Birmingham

Brought up in Bournemouth

British Actor and Comedian

Most Famous for "Hancock's Half Hour"

On BBC Radio and TV

"The trouble with Born-Again Christians is that
they are an even bigger pain the second time around"

"On Fridays a converted cannibal eats only fishermen"

"I prefer to think of them as the Ten Suggestions"

"Adam blamed Eve, Eve blamed the serpent
and the serpent didn't have a leg to stand on"

"It's a bit fishy, that all the apostles were fishermen!"

"Religion's not so bad, unless you believe it,
but my God's godda be better than your god"

Sam Harris

Born 1967

Neuroscientist, Philosopher, Social Critic

Best Selling Author, "The End of Faith"

"Letter to a Christian Nation" etc

"Atheism is really a term we do not need, the same way
that we don't have a word for someone who is not an
astrologer. Everyone was born atheist and all religious
people are atheists with respect to everyone else's religion.
It is difficult to imagine a set of beliefs more suggestive of
mental illness than those that lie at the heart of many
of our religious traditions. I think that religion is the
most dangerous and divisive ideology that we have ever
produced. As it's been protected from criticism, it allows
people to believe en masse, what only idiots or lunatics
could believe in isolation. Pretending to know
things they do not know, is the lifeblood of religion.
Faith is nothing more than the license religious
people give themselves to keep believing
when reasons to believe, fail."

Sam Harris...continued

"The Catholic Church is more concerned about preventing
contraception than preventing child rape;
it's more concerned about preventing
gay marriage than genocide.
This is a real inversion of priorities that completely falsifies
any discussion of morality in the church. Nothing proves the
man-made character of religion as obviously as the sick mind
that designed hell, unless it is the sorely limited mind that has
failed to describe heaven...except as a place of worldly comfort,
eternal tedium, or continual relish in the torture of others.
Imagine a future in which millions of our descendents murder
each other over rival interpretations of Star Wars or
Windows 98. Could anything, anything be more ridiculous?
And yet, this would be no more ridiculous than the world we
are living in. There is no society in human history that ever
suffered because its people became too reasonable. Atheism is
nothing more than a commitment to the most basic standard of
intellectual honesty. The atheist is simply a person who has
perceived the lies of religion and refused to make them his own.
George W Bush says he speaks to Jesus every day, and
Christians love him for it. If George Bush said he spoke to
Jesus through his hair drier, they would think he was mad.
I fail to see how the addition of a hair drier
makes it any more absurd"

Stephen Hawking

Born 1942 in Oxford, England

Graduate of Oxford and Cambridge

Cosmologist and Theoretical Physicist

"I do not believe in a personal God.
My work has shown that you don't have to say that the way the
universe began was the whim of God. The greatest enemy of knowledge
is not ignorance, it is the <u>illusion</u> of knowledge.
The laws of gravity and quantum theory allow universes to appear
spontaneously from nothing. Spontaneous creation is the reason the
universe exists, why we exist. It is not necessary to invoke God to light
the blue touch paper and set the universe going.
I regard the brain as a computer...
there is no heaven or afterlife for broken down computers;
that is a fairy story for people who are afraid of the dark.
There is a fundamental difference between religion, which
is based on authority, and science which is based on observation
and reason. Science will win, because it works.
We could call order by the name of god,
but it would be an impersonal God.
There's not much personal about the laws of physics.
I've noticed even people who claim everything is predestined,
and that we can do nothing to change it,
look before they cross the road!"

Judith Hayes

American Columnist and Writer

"The biblical account of Noah's Ark and the
Flood is perhaps the most implausible story for
fundamentalists to defend.
Where, for example, while loading his ark,
did Noah find
penguins and polar bears in Palestine?
AND
"If we are going to teach creation science as an
alternative to evolution,
then we should teach the Stork theory as
an alternative to biological reproduction"

" I'm not prejudiced against Christianity
I have disdain for _all_ religions!"

Hugh Hefner

Born 1926 in Chicago, Illinois

Playboy Founder, Publisher

and Chief Creative Officer

Since 1953

Bon Vivant and Activist

"The major civilizing force

in the world,

is not religion,

it is SEX"

Robert Heinlein

1907-1988 aged 81

Born in Butler, Missouri

American Science Fiction Writer

"The most preposterous notion ever dreamed up is that the Lord God of Creation, this absurd fantasy, without a shred of evidence, pays all the expenses of the oldest, largest, and least productive industry in all history. Men rarely, if ever, managed to dream up a god superior to themselves. Most gods have the manners and morals of a spoilt child. Theology is never any help; it is searching in a dark cellar at midnight for a black cat that isn't there. But god is omnipotent, omniscient and omnibenevolent. If you have a mind capable of believing all three of these attributes simultaneously...well anyone who can worship a trinity and insist that his religion is a monotheism, can believe anything. One man's Theology is another man's belly laugh!

Joseph Heller

1923-1999 aged 76

Born in Brooklyn, New York

"Decided to live forever,

or die in the attempt"

American Satirical Novelist

and Playwright

Most famous for "Catch 22"

"Good God,

how much reverence can you have for a

Supreme Being

who finds it necessary to include such

phenomena

as phlegm and tooth decay

in his divine system of creation?"

Ernest Hemmingway

1899-1961 aged 62

Born in Chicago, Illinois

Lived in Spain, Cuba,

Key West & Idaho

American Author and Journalist

"For Whom the Bell Tolls" etc

Nobel Prize for Literature in 1954

"All

thinking men are

atheists"

Thor Heyerdahl

1914-2002 aged 88

Born in Larvik, Norway

Norwegian Ethnographer

Zoologist and Adventurer

In 1947, He Sailed Kon-Tiki From

South America to the Tuamotu Islands

And in 1970, He Sailed Ra II

From Morocco to Barbados

"I refrain from having a fixed picture of God.

We have to give up thinking of Him

as an old man with a beard and slippers.

Science can destroy religion

by ignoring it as well as by disproving its tenets.

No one ever demonstrated the non-existence of

Zeus or Thor, but they have very few followers now"

Katherine Hepburn

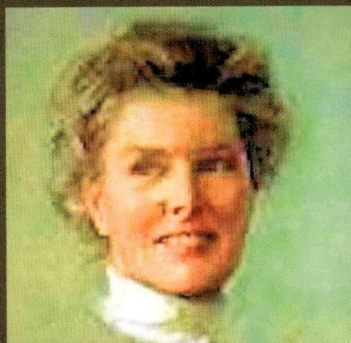

1907-2003 aged 96

Born in Hartford, Connecticut

Academy Award Winning

Star of Stage and Screen

In Her Six Decade Distinguished

Career, She Won Multiple Awards

"I'm an atheist and that's it.
I believe there's nothing we can know,
except that we should be kind
to each other,
and do what we can for other people"

Joe Hillström

1879-1915 aged 36

Born in Gävle, Sweden

Swedish-American Songwriter

Labor Activist and Folk Hero

"Longhaired preachers come out every night,
Tryin' to tell us what's wrong and what's right.
But when asked about somethin' to eat,
They will tell you in voices so sweet
You will eat, you will eat, by and by, by and by
In that glorious land in the sky, way up high
Work and pray, live on hay,
You'll get pie in the sky when you die,
that's a lie"

Brad Hirschfield

Born 1963 in Chicago, Illinois
One of America's Most Influential
Orthodox Rabbis, Author & Lecturer

"Religion
drove those planes into those
buildings. There's no dodging it.
This was done in the name of
religion.
It's amazing how good it is at
mobilizing people to do awful,
murderous things"

Sir Alfred Hitchcock

1899-1980 aged 81

Born in London

British-American Filmmaker & Producer

He was educated at a strict catholic college
in London, where the Jesuit Fathers
were merciless in their beatings

It is said of Hitchcock, the great cinematic
specialist in the art of frightening people, that he
was once driving through Switzerland, when he
suddenly pointed out of the car window and said,
"That is the most frightening sight I have ever seen."
It was a priest in conversation with a little boy,
his hand on the boy's shoulder. Hitchcock
leaned out of the car window and shouted,
"Run, little boy! Run for your life!"

Christopher Hitchens

1949 -2011 aged 62
Born in Portsmouth, Hampshire
Anglo-American Writer & Journalist
His Work Spans Over Four Decades
Author of "God is Not Great" etc

"Religion is poison because it asks us to give up our most precious faculty, which is that of reason, and to believe things without evidence. Then it asks us to respect this, which it calls faith. Gullibility and credulity are considered undesirable qualities in every department of human life, except religion. What can be asserted without evidence can also be dismissed without evidence. Atheism strikes me as morally superior, as well as intellectually superior, to religion. Since it is obviously inconceivable that all religions can be right, the most reasonable conclusion is that they are all wrong. Does this leave us shorn of hope? Not a bit of it. Atheism, and the related conviction that we have just one life to live is the only sure way to regard all our fellow creatures as brothers and sisters. Just consider for a moment what their heaven looks like— Endless praise and adoration...a celestial North Korea"

Adolf Hitler

1889-1945 aged 56

Austrian Born, German Politician, Fascist
Artist, Writer, Nazi Führer, War Criminal

"I am a Catholic and will always remain so.
I am convinced that the people need and require this
faith. We won't allow any other faith to be
promoted. We have undertaken the fight against
the atheistic movement, we have stamped it out.
As for the Jews, I am just carrying on with the same
policy which the Catholic Church has adopted for
1,500 years. I am convinced that I am acting as the
agent of our Almighty Creator. By fighting the
Jews, I am doing the Lord's work. The work that
Christ started but could not finish, I, Adolf Hitler,
will conclude. Thus inwardly armed with
confidence in God, and the unshakable stupidity of
the citizenry, the politicians can begin the fight"

Oliver Wendell Holmes

1841-1935 aged 94

Born in Boston, Massachusetts

Justice of the Supreme Court

of the United States 1902-1932

"Men are idolaters, and want something to
look at and kiss, and throw themselves down
before, and if you don't make it of wood, you
must make it of words. The truth is that the
whole system of beliefs which comes with the
story of the fall of man is gently falling out
of enlightened human intelligence.
The man who is always worrying whether or
not his soul would be damned, generally has
a soul that isn't worth a damn"

George Holyoake

1817-1906 aged 89

Born in Birmingham, England

Philosopher, Lecturer

Writer, Reformer

"I do not believe there is such

a thing as

a God"

In 1842, He was

The Last Englishman

to be <u>Imprisoned</u>

for Being an Atheist!

Bob Hoskins

As Smee in "Hook"

Born 1942 in Bury St Edmunds

Suffolk

English Cockney Actor

On Stage Screen and TV

Brought up as an atheist

but now describes himself

as an agnostic

"Acting is my religion!"

Ed Howe

1853-1937 aged 84

American Novelist and Editor

"None of us can boast about the morality of our ancestors. The records do <u>not</u> show that Adam and Eve were married"!

Picture from the Creation Museum, Kentucky

Sir Fred Hoyle

1915-2001 aged 86

Born in Gilstead, Yorkshire

English Astronomer, Mathematician

and Science Fiction Writer

"Religion
is but a desperate attempt to find an
escape from the truly dreadful situation in
which we find ourselves. Here we are in this wholly
fantastic universe with scarcely a clue as whether
or not our existence has in fact, any real
significance.
No wonder then, that so many people feel the need
for some belief that gives them a sense of security,
and no wonder that they become very
angry with people like me who say
that this is illusory"

Elbert Hubbard

1856-1915 aged 59

Born in Bloomington, Illinois

Writer, Publisher, Artist & Philosopher

"A MIRACLE is an event described by those
to whom it was told, by people who didn't see it.
ORTHODOXY is that peculiar condition where the
patient can neither eliminate an old idea,
nor absorb a new one.
It is a corpse that doesn't know it's dead.
DOGMA is a lie reiterated and authoritatively injected
into the mind of one or more persons who believe that they
believe what someone else believes.
THEOLOGY is an attempt to explain a subject by men
who do not understand it. The intent is not to tell the
truth, but to satisfy the questioner.
FAITH is the effort to believe what your common sense
tells you is not true.
SINS, we are punished <u>by</u> our sins, not for them"

L Ron Hubbard

1911-1986 aged 75

Born in Tilden, Nebraska
American Science Fiction Writer
Religious Leader Who in 1952 Founded
The Church of Scientology
and Self Help System called Dianetics
"Writing for a penny a word is ridiculous. If a man
wants to make a million dollars, the best way is to
start a new religion. Religion is a hoax to control people.
I achieved my own ends beautifully, I orientated myself
in the world, recognized what was important and what
was not. I defined for my own use, such things as
morality and evil and ethics in general, and established
what satisfied me as being the true psychology and
religion "He portrayed himself as an explorer, world
traveler, nuclear physicist, photographer, artist,
poet and philosopher. His critics characterize him
as a liar, a charlatan and a madman

Mike Huckabee

Born 1955 in Hope, Arkansas

Former Heavy Weight Governor of Arkansas

from 1996 to 2007

A Creationist and

Southern Baptist Minister

Possible Presidential Contender in 2012

"To separate politics from religion is
impossible. I believe it's a lot easier to change
the Constitution than it would be to change
the word of the living God, and that's what
we need to do is to amend the Constitution so
it's in God's standards rather than try to
change God's standards.

Regarding Obama, one thing I do know
is that he was raised in Kenya"

IN FACT HE WAS RAISED IN HAWAII & INDONESIA!

Victor Hugo

1802-1885 aged 83

Born in Besançon, France

Lived Mostly in Jersey and Guernsey

French Poet, Dramatist, Novelist

"Les Misérables" etc

Artist, Human Rights Activist & Statesman

"There is in every village a torch:

the schoolmaster

and an extinguisher:

the parson.

There shall be no slavery of the mind.

Every step which the intelligence

of Europe has taken,

has been in spite of the clergy"

David Hume

1711-1776 aged 65

Born in Edinburgh, Scotland

Philosopher, Historian, Economist & Essayist

As an Atheist, he was Barred

from the Chair of Philosophy

at Glasgow University

"When I hear a man is religious,
I conclude that he is a rascal,
although I have known some instances
of very good men being religious"

"Examine the religious principles which
have prevailed in the world, and you will
scarcely be persuaded that they are
anything but sick men's dreams"

John Humphrys

Born 1943 in Cardiff, Wales

Award Winning Radio & TV Presenter

Journalist & Author of "In God We Doubt"

"I used to be a Christian, I'm now a devout skeptic, a
failed atheist, with lots of Big Questions but no Big
Answers. After a lifetime of puzzling over an insoluble
conundrum,
I'm not prepared to say there's nothing there.
I do believe there's something there.
What the hell it is I have absolutely no idea!
But to suggest, as Dawkins and Hitchens do,
that religion is the greatest evil,
the greatest danger, the greatest threat
the world faces, is simply nonsense.
There is no historical justification for that claim"
REALLY?

Zora Neale Hurston

1891-1960 aged 69

Born in Notasulga, Alabama

Folklorist, Anthropologist

Novelist, Essayist

& Playwright

"Gods
always behave
like the people
who created them!"

John Huston

1906-1987 aged 81

Born in Nevada, Missouri

Distinguished Hollywood Film Director

"The Maltese Falcon" "African Queen"

"Treasure of Sierra Madre" & "Key Largo"

"You walk through a series of arches,
so to speak, and then, at the end of the
corridor, a door opens and you see backward
through time, and you feel the flow of time,
and you realize you are only part of a great
nameless procession... I prefer to think
God is not dead...just dead drunk"

Aldous Huxley

1894-1963 aged 69

Born in Godalming, Surrey
Lived in Los Angeles his last 26 years
Writer, Humanist and Pacifist

"Single-mindedness is all very well in cows
or baboons; in an animal claiming to belong to
the same species as Shakespeare it is simply
disgraceful. Facts do not cease to exist because
they are ignored. You never see animals going
through the absurd and often horrible fooleries of
magic and religion. Only man behaves with
such gratuitous folly. It is the price he has to
pay for being intelligent but not, as yet,
quite intelligent enough"

Sir Julian Huxley

1887-1975 aged 88

Born in London

Brother of Aldous

Evolutionary Biologist

Humanist and Internationalist

Founding Member of the World Wild Life Fund

"We should be agnostic about those things for which there is no evidence. We should not hold beliefs merely because they gratify our desires for afterlife, immortality, heaven and hell etc.

Gods, angels, demons, and spirits are a human product, arising from a certain kind of ignorance and a certain degree of helplessness with respect to man's external environment. God is beginning to resemble not a ruler, but the last fading smile of a cosmic Cheshire cat"

Robert Ingersoll

1833-1899 aged 66

Born in Dresden, New York

Political Leader, Civil War Veteran & Orator

Agnostic son of a Presbyterian Preacher

"Religion has not civilized man, man has civilized religion"

"As people become more intelligent
they will care less for preachers, and more for teachers"

"The few have said, Think!
The many have said, Believe!"

"The inspiration of the bible
depends on the ignorance of the person who reads it"

"Our ignorance is God; what we know, is science"

"Ignorance is the soil in which belief in miracles grows"

"Why should I allow the same God to tell me
how to raise my kids, who had to drown his own"

"The man who does not do his own thinking is a slave,
and is a traitor to himself and to his fellow-men"

Michelangelo..painted some angels wearing sandals.
A cardinal said 'Whoever saw angels wearing sandals?!
The artist replied: "Who ever saw an angel barefooted?

The clergy know, I know, that they know, that they do not know"

Robert Ingersoll...continued

All that is necessary to convince any reasonable person that the Bible is simply and purely of human invention, of barbarian invention, is to read it. Read it as you would any other book; think of it as you would of any other; get the bandage of reverence from your eyes; drive from your heart the phantom of fear; push from the throne of your brain any form of superstition, then read the Holy Bible and you will be amazed that you ever, for one moment, supposed a being of infinite wisdom, goodness and purity, to be the author of such ignorance and of such atrocity. Every religion in the world has declared every other religion a fraud. That is the time all religions tell the truth. If a man would follow, today, the teachings of the Old Testament, he would be a criminal. If he would follow the teachings of the New Testament, he would be insane. Our Constitution was framed, not to declare and uphold the deity of Christ, but the sacredness of humanity. Ours is the first government made by the people and for the people. It is the only nation with which the gods have had nothing to do. And yet there are some judges dishonest and cowardly enough to solemnly decide that this is a Christian country, and that our free institutions are based upon the infamous laws of Jehovah. The church has always been willing to swap off treasures in heaven for cash down!"
Take from the Church the miraculous, the supernatural, the incomprehensible, the impossible, the unknowable, the absurd ...and nothing but a vacuum remains!"

Eddie Izzard

Born 1962 in Aden, Yemen

British Comedian and Actor

"The Crusades were:

We kill you in the name of Jesus!"

"Wait, <u>we</u> have Jesus too! He's a prophet in our religion! <u>We</u> kill <u>you</u> in the name of Jesus!"

"Do you? Well, we kill you for your dark skin, for Jesus was a white man from Oxford!"

"No, he wasn't! He was from Judea! A dark-skinned man, such as we!"

"Really? Look we've come all this way. Would you mind awfully if we hacked you to bits? Just for the press back home"

A J Jacobs

Born 1968 in New York City

Best Selling Author

and Journalist

"The-Know-It-All"

"The Year of Living Biblically"

"My Life as an Experiment" etc

Studied Philosophy

at Brown University

"I am officially Jewish,

but I'm Jewish in the same way

The Olive Garden is an Italian restaurant.

I'm still agnostic, but I'm

a reverent agnostic"

Clive James

Born 1939 in Sydney, Australia

Even as a Child His IQ was 140

Studied Psychology at Sydney University

Lived and Worked in England Since 1962

Wit, Journalist, Memoirist, Atheist Author,

Critic, Poet, Broadcaster

TV Talk Show Host

Reads French, German, Italian, Spanish,

Russian, Japanese, Latin and Greek!

"Religions

are advertising agencies

for a product

that doesn't exist!"

Thomas Jefferson

1743-1826 aged 83

Born in Albemarle County, Virginia

3rd president of the United States 1801-1809

Principal Author of

the Declaration of Independence, 1776

Encouraged Lewis and Clark to explore the Far West

Interestingly, he and John Adams of course,

both signed the Declaration of Independence

on 4th July 1776—both died on 4th July 1826!

Exactly fifty years later!

"Christianity is the most perverted system that ever shone on
man, I do not find one redeeming feature.
Religions are all alike, founded upon fables and mythology.
In every country and every age,
the priest had been hostile to Liberty. He is always
in alliance with the despot, abetting his abuses
in return for protection to his own abuses.
The Christian God is cruel, vindictive, capricious and unjust.
One only needs to look at the caliber of people who say they
serve him. They are always of two classes: fools and hypocrites"

Penn

Gillette

Of "Penn and Teller"

Born 1955

in Greenfield

Massachusetts

Illusionist

Entertainer

Activist

"Read the Bible,

we need

more atheists!"

Billy Joel

Born 1949 in The Bronx, New York

Recording Star, Entertainer, Pianist

Composer, Singer-Songwriter, 33 Top Hits

Has sold Over 150 Million Records

"Honesty is such a lonely word,

everyone is so untrue"

"I wasn't raised Catholic, but I used to go to Mass
with friends. I viewed it as enthralling hocus-pocus.
There's this guy on the wall in the church, nailed to
a cross and dripping blood, and everybody's blaming
themselves for that man's torment, but I said to
myself, Forget it. I had no hand in that evil.
There's no blood of any sacred martyr on my hands.
I pass on all this. I had some Jewish guilt in me
already, so I had no room for Catholic guilt too"

Sir Elton John

Born 1947 in Pinner, Middlesex

Recording Star, Pianist, Composer

Singer-Songwriter and Activist

Has Sold Over 250 Million Records!

"I would ban all religions.

Religion fuels anti-gay discrimination.

It promotes hatred and spite against gays.

From my point of view, I would ban religion

completely, it turns people into hateful

lemmings and it's not really compassionate.

And why can't they have gays in the

military? Personally, I think it's because

they're afraid of a thousand gay guys with

guns, going 'Who you calling a faggot?'!"

Pope John Paul

1920-2005 aged 85

Born in Wadwice, Poland

Reigned as Pope from 1978 to 2005

He spoke Polish, Italian, French

German, English, Spanish, Portuguese, Ukrainian,

Russian, Croatian, Esperanto, Greek and Latin!

"New knowledge has led to the recognition in

The Theory of Evolution

of more than a hypothesis. It is indeed remarkable
that this theory has been progressively accepted by
researchers, following a series of discoveries in various
fields of knowledge. The convergence, neither sought
nor fabricated, of the results of work that was
conducted independently, is in itself a significant
argument in favor of this theory"

Ellen Johnson

Has Degrees in Environmental

Studies and Political Science

Describes herself as a

Second Generation

Atheist

She has been Active in

American Atheists

since 1978 and

was their President from

1995 to 2008

Philip Johnson

1906-2005 aged 99

Born in Cleveland, Ohio

Elder Statesman of American Architects

He Studied Philosophy and Architecture

at Harvard

In 1930 He Founded the Department of Architecture

and Design at New York's Museum of Modern Art

In His 99 Years He Produced

Many Memorable Buildings:

The Glass House, The Seagram Building

The AT&T/Sony Building

Inter Faith Peace Chapel,

The Chapel of Thanksgiving

and the Chrystal Cathedral

"He wasn't a person of faith

but he was a person of great vision"

Phillip E Johnson

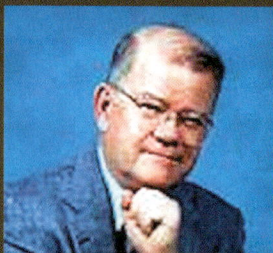

Born 1940 in Aurora, Illinois
Later, Born Again
Studied English Literature at Harvard
and Law at the University of Chicago
Retired Berkley Law Professor
and Author of "Darwin on Trial"
While on Sabbatical in England
He Prayed, Asking What He Should Do
With the Rest of His Life, and was Told to
Combat Darwinism, and so, After Reading
Richard Dawkins' Books
He Became the Father of Devine Design
and Prominent Critic of Evolution
and an AIDS Denialist

Angelina Jolie

Born 1975 in Los Angeles

California

Hollywood Film Star

and Activist

"Is there a

God?

For people who believe

in it,

I hope so!"

Pastor Terry Jones

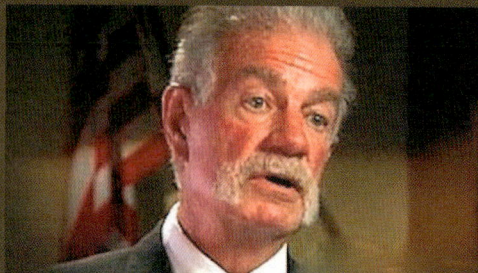

Born 1953, Later, Born Again

Fundamentalist Christian

of Gainesville, Florida

He Burned the Koran

on 20th March 2011

Causing Deadly Protests

in Afghanistan in

Which Over 20 People

Have Been Killed

and Many More Injured.

...RELIGIOUS HATRED

James Joyce

1882-1941 aged 59

Born Near Dublin, Ireland

Irish Novelist and Poet

He was to Modern Literature

What Picasso was to Modern Art

"There is no heresy or no philosophy which

is so abhorrent to the Church

as a human being"

"Broken heart. A pump after all,

pumping thousands of gallons of

blood every day. One fine day it gets

bunged up..and once you are

dead you are dead"

Joachim Kahl

Born 1941 in Cologne, Germany
Philosopher and author of
"The Misery of Christianity:
A Plea for Humanity without God"

"What after all is the cross of Jesus Christ?
It is nothing but the sum total of a
sadomasochistic glorification of pain.
Christianity has not failed the ideals of its
founder: Christ has failed. Corrupt in its
very essence, the gospel of Christ alone has
persecuted Jews, defamed the female and
suppressed sexuality"
FOR PROOF, SEE MEL GIBSON'S FILM
"THE PASSION OF CHRIST"

Franklin E Kameny

1925-2011 aged 86

Born in New York City

American Astronomer

Atheist and Gay Rights Activist

Since Being Dismissed in 1957 from the

Army Map Service for Being Homosexual.

He has Fought Church Doctrine and

Federal Law to Achieve Civil Rights

for Gays and Lesbians.

An example of religious vilification from the

Reverend Jerry Falwell; "Homosexuals are

brute beasts...part of a vile Satanic System

that will be utterly annihilated and there

will be a celebration in heaven"

Emmanuel Kant

1724-1804 aged 80

Born in Königsberg, Prussia

Writer, Lecturer and Researcher

Professor of Philosophy at Königsberg

"Have courage
to use your own reason!
That is the motto of
enlightenment.
He who has made great
moral progress
ceases to pray"

Diane Keaton

Born 1946 in Los Angeles, California

Hollywood Film Star Since 1970

Also Stage Actress, Singer,

Screenwriter, Director, Producer,

Photographer

and Property Developer

"I used to be Methodist

then agnostic

but now I'm

an atheist"

John Keats

1779-1821 aged 42

Born in London

Lived in Hampstead and Rome

English Romantic Poet

Along with Lord Byron and Shelly

"I have been astonished

That men could die martyrs

for their religion

I have shudder'd at it

I shudder no more.

I could be martyr'd for my religion

Love is my religion

And I could die for that

I could die for you"

"Truth, beauty. Beauty, truth.

That is all you need to know in life.

That is all you'll ever need to know"

Garrison Keillor

Born 1942 in Anoka, Minnesota

Author, Storyteller, Humorist

Radio Personality and Film Star

Most Famous Since 1971 for NPR's

"A Prairie Home Companion"

Which was also a Movie in 2007

"My ancestors were Puritans from England.
They arrived here in 1648 in hopes of finding
greater restrictions than were permissible under
English law at that time! We come from people who
brought us up to believe that life is a struggle, and
if you should feel happy, be patient: this will pass!
God writes a lot of comedy...the trouble is he's stuck
with so many bad actors who don't know how to
play funny. It is a sin to believe evil of others,
but it is seldom a mistake!"

Gene Kelly

1912-1996 aged 84

Born in Pittsburgh, Pennsylvania

Stage and Movie Star

Dancer, Choreographer, Actor, Singer

Film Director and Producer

Known for His Athletic Dancing Style

Academy Honorary Award in 1952

Young Gene, driving through Mexico, seeing
the poverty of the peasants, and the Catholic
churches, rich with gold and silver and jewels.
Sickened by the contrast, it opened his eyes to
the hypocrisy of organized religion, and he made
it plain to his father, that he was now
a complete agnostic.

Helen Keller

1880-1968 aged 88

Born in Tuscumbia, Alabama

Blind and Deaf

Socialist, Pacifist and Suffragist.

At One and a Half, Meningitis or Scarlet Fever

Left Her Deaf and Blind. But she became the First

Deafblind Person to Earn a Bachelor of Art Degree

"There is much in the Bible against which every instinct of my being rebels, so much that I regret the necessity which has compelled me to read it from beginning to end. I do not think that the knowledge which I have gained of its history and sources compensates me for the unpleasant details it forced upon my attention. Good people spend so much time fighting the devil. If they would only expend the same amount of energy loving their fellow men, the devil would die of boredom"

John F Kennedy

1917-1963 aged 46

Born in Brookline, Massachusetts

35th President of the United States

from 1961 to 1963...

When He was Assassinated in Dallas,

Texas on 22nd November

by Lee Harvey Oswald

"I believe in an America where

religious intolerance will someday end,

where every man has the same

right to attend or not attend

the church of his choice"

Sir Ludovic Kennedy

1919-2009 aged 90

Born in Edinburgh, Scotland
British Broadcaster, Author
Journalist, Humanist and Activist

"God is a human invention,
a fictional character...like Hamlet.
Intelligent Christians must know that prayers
go unanswered. If it were otherwise, every
non-believer in the land would convert to
Christianity tomorrow. So why do Christians
continue to pray, pray?
A poll of 15,000 British school children found that a
third called themselves agnostics, and a quarter said
they were atheists. That adds up to
non-believers being a majority"

Jomo Kenyatta

1894-1978 aged 84

Born in Gatundu, Kenya

1st Prime Minister of Kenya 1963- 1964

Then 1st President of Kenya 1964-1978

"When the missionaries arrived,
the Africans had the Land
and the Missionaries had the Bible.
They taught us to pray with our eyes closed.
When we opened them,
they had the land
and we had the Bible"

THIS SAME QUOTE IS ALSO ATTRIBUTED TO
ARCHBISHOP DESMOND TUTU

John Kerry

Born 1943 in Aurora, Colorado

United States Senator from Massachusetts

Chairman of the Foreign Relations

Committee

In 2004 He Lost by Just

34 Electoral Votes

to George W Bush

Viet Nam War Hero, Attorney

"I can't take my Catholic belief,
my article of faith, and legislate it on
a Protestant, or a Jew or an Atheist.
We have separation of church and state,
in the United States of America"

Omar Khayyám

1048-1131 aged 83

Born in Neyshapur, Persia

Astronomer, Philosopher, Poet, Mathematician

Teacher of Mechanics, Geography & Music

"Oh Threats of Hell and hopes of Paradise!

One thing at least is certain - This life flies;

One thing is certain and the rest is lies;

The flower that once has blown forever dies.

And if the wine you drink, the lip you press,

End in the nothing all things end in - Yes

Then fancy while thou art, thou art but what

Thou shalt be - nothing - thou shalt not be less"

Ayatollah Khomeini

1902-1989 aged 87

Born in Nishapur, Iran

Iranian Religious Leader & Politician

Leader of the 1979 Iranian Revolution

Which Overthrew The Shah.

"There is no room for play in Islam...
It is deadly serious about everything.
Americans are the great Satan.
All those against the revolution must
disappear and quickly be executed."

THERE ARE OTHER QUOTES ATTRIBUTED TO THE
AYATOLLAH, TOO HORRIFIC TO INCLUDE HERE

Martin Luther King Jr

1929-1968 aged 39

Born in Atlanta, Georgia

Baptist Minister, Activist and Leader of

the African American Civil Rights Movement

Using Gandhi's Non-Violent Methods.

In 1963 He Lead the March on Washington

where King delivered His

'I Have a Dream' Speech.

He was Assassinated in Memphis, Tennessee.

"Nothing in the world is more dangerous than

sincere ignorance and conscientious stupidity.

He who passively accepts evil is as much

involved in it as he who helps to perpetrate it.

He who accepts evil without protesting against

it, is really cooperating with it"

Stephen King

Born 1947 in Portland, Maine
Author of Contemporary Horror,
Suspense and Science Fiction.
His Books Have Sold Over
350 Million Copies!

"The beauty of religious mania
is that it has the power to explain
everything. Once God (or Satan) is
accepted as the first cause of everything
which happens in the mortal world,
nothing is left to chance...logic can be
happily tossed out the window"

Alfred Kinsey

1894-1956 aged 62

Born in Hoboken, New Jersey

Biologist, Professor of Entomology and Zoology.

Founder in 1947 Of the Groundbreaking Kinsey

Institute of Sex Research at Indiana University.

Known as the Father of Sexology,

He Published in 1948

"The Sexual Behavior of the Human Male"

and in 1953

"The Sexual Behavior of the Human Female."

He was Raised by Very Strict Methodist Parents

and Was Forbidden by His Father to Learn

Anything About the Very Subject That

Was Later to Bring Him Such Fame.

Ultimately, He Disavowed Christianity,

and Became an Atheist.

Louis Kronenberger

1904-1980 aged 76

Cincinnati, Ohio

New York Theater Critic and Author

Drama Critic for Time Magazine

from 1938 to 1961 and

Theater Arts Professor

"There seems to be a terrible
misunderstanding on the part of a
great many people, to the effect that
when you cease to believe,
you may cease to behave"

Stanley Kubrick

1928-1999 aged 71

Born in Manhattan, New York
Film Director, Producer, Writer and Photographer
"Spartacus" "Lolita" "Barry Lyndon"
"Dr Strangelove" "A Clockwork Orange"
"2001 Space Odyssey" "Eyes Wide Shut"
"I don't think there's a God and I don't believe in hell. The most
terrifying fact about the universe is not that it's hostile, but
that it's indifferent; but if we can come to terms with this
indifference, and accept the challenges of life within the
boundaries of death..our existence as a species can have
genuine meaning and fulfillment. However vast the darkness,
we must supply our own light. I'd be very surprised if the
universe wasn't full of an intelligence of an order that to us
would seem God-like. There are approximately 100 billion stars
in our galaxy alone, and approximately 100 billion galaxies in
just the visible Universe...so it seems likely that there are
billions of planets in the universe..where intelligent life ..is
hundreds of thousands or millions of years in advance of
us...and their intelligence ungraspable by humans"

Osama bin Laden

1957-2011 aged 54

Born in Saudi Arabia, 17th child of over 50 siblings of
a wealthy Islamic family, he became the most wanted
fanatical fundamentalist terrorist leader, who plotted
and funded the attacks that killed nearly 3,000 on 9/11.
On 1st May 2011, he was shot and killed in a daring US raid, not
in a cave, but in his mansion in Pakistan. President Bush
had vowed to capture or kill bin Laden, but 9 months later
said "I truly am not that concerned about him" And he closed
the unit hunting for him. Bush had nearly 3,000 days to get
the villain. President Obama accomplished it, showing great
guts, in 820 days. Bin Laden didn't dare use technology for
contacts, so he had couriers, and the CIA tracked one to the
hide-out. So Osama bin Laden and Adolf Hitler, both of them
"very religious", one a Muslim extremist, the other
a Roman Catholic extremist...each of them
died by gunshot, on the 1st May, 66 years apart.
THERE'S A RUMOR THAT HIS LAST WORDS WERE "O BUMMER"

Anne Lamott

Born 1954 in San Francisco,

California

Novelist and Non-Fiction Writer

Political Activist, Public Speaker

And Writing Teacher

"You can safely assume that

you've created God

in your own image,

when it turns out that he or she

hates all the same people you do"

Mick LaSalle

Born in 1959

Film Critic for the

San Francisco Chronicle

"He talked about Father Junípero
Serra's qualifications for sainthood:
They say he cured a nun's lupus.
A miracle. Now I'm not a doctor, but
I know lupus goes into remission.
It's not always fatal. Have
Ray Charles and Stevie Wonder
play ping-pong together.
That's a miracle"

Hugh Laurie

Born 1959 in Oxford, England

English Comedian and Actor

Writer, Musician, Director

and Recording Artist

American TV Star

"I'm

an atheist,

religion is

man-made"

D H Lawrence

1885-1930 aged 45

Born in Nottingham, England
English Novelist, Poet, Playwright, Essayist &
Literary Critic. Famous for "Sons and Lovers'
"Women in Love" etc, and thanks to
"Lady Chatterley's Lover" He was Labeled a
Pornographer! He Escaped England at the Earliest
Opportunity, and Traveled for the Rest of His Life,
Living in Australia, Italy, Ceylon, America,
Mexico and the South of France.
"God is a great imaginative experience.
I know the greatness of Christianity,
it is a past greatness.
Be a good animal,
true to your animal instincts"

Lynn Lavner

Born in Brooklyn, New York

Jewish, Lesbian Comedian

"America's Most
Politically Incorrect Entertainer!"

"The Bible
contains 6 admonitions to homosexuals
and 362 admonitions to heterosexuals.
That doesn't mean God doesn't love
heterosexuals.
It's just that they need more
supervision!"

Richard Leaky

Born 1944 in Nairobi, Kenya
Paleoanthropologist & Conservationist
And Kenyan Politician

"I've been raised to believe in freedom of thought and
speech. The fruits of intellectual and technological
endeavor give us just an inkling of what the
human mind can achieve. The potential is
enormous, almost infinite.
We are lucky that the earth's history is recorded in
fossilized remains. And we can see the changes, there
is no doubt that we, and everything living today,
has evolved.
What is strange, is that there are still
people who believe the world is not a globe"

Richard Lederer

Born in 1938

American Author, Speaker
Teacher and Linguist
Best Known for His Over 35 Books
on English Language, Wordplay
and Use of Oxymorons
Describes Himself as a Verbivore.

"There once was a time when all people
believed in God and the Church ruled.
This time was called
The Dark Ages"

Tom Lehrer

Born 1928 in Manhattan, New York

Singer-songwriter, Satirist, Pianist

Mathematician & Harvard Lecturer

"First you get down on your knees,

Fiddle with your rosaries,

Bow your head with great respect,

And genuflect, genuflect, genuflect!

Do whatever steps you want if

You have cleared them with the Pontiff

Get in line in that processional

Step into that small confessional,

There, the guy who's got religion'll

Tell you if your sin's original.

If it is, try playin' it safer,

Drink the wine and chew the wafer.

Make a cross on your abdomen,

When in Rome, do like a Roman,

Ave Maria,

Gee, it's good to see ya,

Getting' exstatic an'

Sorta dramatic an'

Doin' the Vatican Rag!"

Bruce Lee

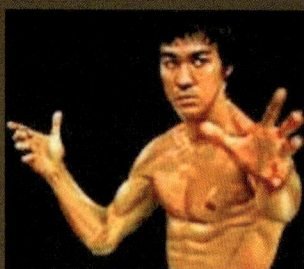

1940-1973 aged 33

Born in San Francisco

Fighting Film Star

Hong Kong Film Actor

Director and Producer

Screen Writer & Philosopher

"I have no religious affiliation.

None whatsoever.

To be perfectly frank,

I do not believe in God

I believe in sleeping!"

Gypsy Rose Lee

1911-1970 aged 59

Born in Seattle, Washington

American Burlesque Entertainer

Famous for her Striptease Act.

Broadway and Film Musicals

Have Been Made of Her Memoirs

"God is love, but get it in writing"
"Praying is like a rocking chair—
it gives you something to do,
but it won't get you anywhere"

Vladimir Lenin

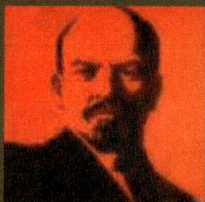

1870-1924 aged 54

Born in Simbirsk, Russia

Russian Marxist Revolutionary,
Author, Lawyer, Economist, Philosopher
and Creator of the Soviet Communist Party

"Religion is one of the forms of spiritual
oppression which everywhere weighs down
heavily upon the masses of the people.
Autocracy cannot do without its twin
agents: a hangman and a priest, the first to
suppress popular resistance by force, the
second to sweeten the lot of the oppressed with
empty promises of a heavenly kingdom.
Rational arguments don't work
with religious people"

John Lennon

1940-1980 aged 40

Born in Liverpool, England

Shot to Death in New York

Musician, Singer-songwriter and Activist

World Famous as a Founding

Member of the Beatles

"Imagine there's no heaven,

It's easy if you try.

No hell below us,

Above us only sky.

Imagine all the people,

Living for today..

Imagine there's no countries,

It isn't hard to do.

Nothing to kill or die for,

And no religion too"

Pope Leo X

1475-1521 aged 46

Born in Florence, Italy

Reigned as Pope from 1513 to 1521

Known for Selling Indulgences

& His Conflict with Martin

Luther

"It has served us well,

this myth of

Christ"

Pope Leo XIII

1810-1903 aged 93

Born Near Rome, Italy

He Reigned from 1878 to 1903

"The death sentence
is a necessary and efficacious
means for the Church to attain
its ends, when obstinate heretics
disturb the ecclesiastical order.
The equal toleration of all
religions is the same as atheism"

C S Lewis

1898-1963 aged 65

Born in Belfast, Northern Ireland

British Novelist, Medievalist, Essayist,
Academic & Literary Critic

"Of all bad men,
religious bad men are the worst.
Christianity, if false is of no importance,
and if true, of infinite importance.
The only thing it can't be
is of moderate importance"

Joseph Lewis

1889-1968 aged 79

Born in Montgomery, Alabama

Publisher, Freethinker & Atheist

"There are no bended knees in atheism,
no prayers, no "divine" revelations,
no crusades, no massacres, no holy wars,
no heaven, no hell, no purgatory,
no silly rewards, no vindictive punishments,
no Christs, no devils, and no gods.
Atheism is a vigorous and courageous,
self-reliant philosophy,
a passionate search for truth"

Sinclair Lewis

1885-1951 aged 66

Born in Sauk Centre, Minnesota

American Novelist & Short Story Writer

First American Writer to be

Awarded the Nobel Prize for Literature

"It is a mistake to believe that there is any
need for religion to make life... worth living.
When fanaticism comes to America,
it will be wrapped in a flag
and carrying a cross"

Rush Limbaugh

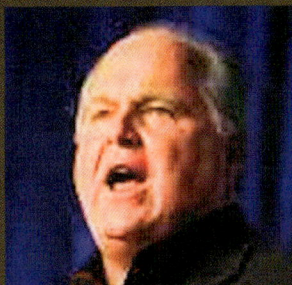

Born 1951 in Cape Girardeau, Missouri

American Radio Talk Show Host

Conservative, Republican

Political Commentator

Makes Fifty Million Dollars a Year!

"If you don't believe in God, you have no meaning in your life, and you will search for meaning, and find it anywhere. Most people, even atheists want religion of some kind in their life. Hello, Global Warming as a substitute! The global warming people essentially are atheists. You cannot believe in the God of Creation and believe manmade global warming. "I don't want to destroy God's creation" God's laughing at you! You can't! He could, but you can't. You can't create it; you can't destroy it"

Abraham Lincoln

1809-1865 aged 56

Born in a one-room log cabin in Kentucky

An avid reader, he was mostly self-educated

16th President of the United States

From 1861 to his assassination in March 1865

"The Bible is not my book, nor Christianity my religion, I could never give assent to the long, complicated statements of Christian dogma. My earlier views of the unsoundness of the Christian scheme of salvation and the human origin of the scriptures, have become clearer and stronger with advancing years. It will not do to investigate the subject of religion too closely, as it is apt to lead to infidelity. You can fool some of the people all of the time, and all of the people some of the time, but you cannot fool all of the people all of the time"

Louis XIV

The Palace of Versailles   1638-1715 aged 76

Born in Chateau de Saint Germain en Laye, France

Known as The Sun King, He Reigned

for 72 years from the Age of 4!

He made the Palace at Versailles the

Largest, Grandest Palace in the World!

A Devout Catholic, He Revoked the Edict of

Nantes Which had Given Religious Tolerance to

the Huguenots, Who Were Then Forced to

Convert to Catholicism or Go to Prison.

Many Emigrated. When He was Told of a

Defeat in a Battle, He Said

"Has God forgotten all I have done for Him?"

St Ignatius Loyola

1491-1556 aged 65

Born in Azpeitia, Spain

Priest, Theologian and Hermit

Founder of The Society of Jesus

...The Jesuits

"We should always be disposed to
believe that which appears to us to be
white, is really black,
if the Hierarchy of The Church
so decides"

Lucretius

94 BC-55 BC aged 39

Born In Rome, Italy

Roman Poet and Philosopher

Wrote the Epic Poem

"On the Nature of the Universe"

"Rest, brother, rest, have you done ill or well.

Rest, rest, there is no God, no gods do dwell.

Crowned with avenging righteousness on high.

Nor frowning ministers of their hate in hell.

Fear is the mother of all gods.

Too often in time past, religion has brought forth

criminal and shameful actions.

How many evils have religions caused?

All religions are equally sublime to the ignorant,

Useful to the politician,

and ridiculous to the philosopher.

Martin Luther

1483-1546 aged 63

Born in Eisenleben, Germany

Then Part of the Holy Roman Empire.

German Priest and Professor of Theology

Initiator of the Protestant Reformation

Was Excommunicated by Pope Leo X

"Whoever wants to be a Christian, should tear out the eyes of his reason. Reason is a whore, the greatest enemy that faith has. Faith must trample underfoot, all reason, sense and understanding. Know nothing but the Word of God. We must drive Jews out like mad dogs, so we do not become partakers of their abominable blasphemy and all their other vices, and thus merit God's wrath, and be damned with them"

Seth MacFarlane

Born 1973 in Kent, Connecticut

Animator, Actor, Voice Actor, Writer, Comedian, Singer,

Director, Producer & Creator of Family Guy etc

"Religion claims that they invented morality.
They didn't.
I do not believe in God. I'm an atheist.
I consider myself a free thinker, and it fascinates me
that in the 21st century most people still believe in
'the invisible man in the sky'.
I'm an atheist, not to be a dick,
but just because it seems like the most likely scenario. If
you say "There's a monster in my closet, you can't see
him, but you gotta have faith that he's there".
People would say "Well that's ridiculous, you're out of
your mind, you should be locked up," but the same thing
does not apply to a guy living on a cloud"

James Madison

1751-1836 aged 85

Born in Belle Grove Plantation, Virginia
One of the Founding Fathers.
Principle Author of the US Constitution
4th President of the United States 1809-1817
In 1803, He Supervised The Louisiana Purchase
From France for $15 M, Doubling the US Size

"What has been Christianity's fruits?
Superstition, Bigotry and Persecution.
Religious bondage shackles and debilitates the mind
and unfits it for every noble enterprise.
Ecclesiastical establishments tend to great
ignorance and corruption, all of which facilitate
the execution of mischievous projects.
<u>When tyranny comes to this land,
it will be in the guise of fighting a foreign foe"</u>

Ferdinand Magellan

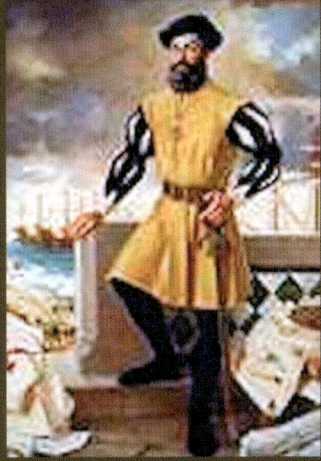

1480-1521 aged 41

Born in Sabrosa, Portugal

Portuguese Explorer

The First European to Sail Across

Both the Atlantic and Pacific Oceans

Thus Circumnavigating the Earth

Via Cape Horn and the Cape of Good Hope

"The Church says the Earth is flat,
but I know that it is round, for I have seen
the shadow on the moon, and I have more
faith in a shadow than in the Church"

Bill Maher

Born 1956 in New York City

Award Winning Stand-Up Comedian
TV Host, Political Commentator ,Satirist, Author, Actor,
Filmmaker of "Religulous!" A Liberal, With a Capital L!
With a Lapsed Catholic Father and a Lapsed Jewish Mother!"
"To call atheism a religion
is like calling abstinence a sex position!
Religion is dangerous because it allows people who don't have all
the answers, to think that they do. That is why rational people,
anti-religionists, must end their timidity and come out of their
closets and assert themselves. We are a nation that is
unenlightened because of religion, it stops people thinking.
Flying planes into buildings was a faith-based initiative. I think
religion is a neurological disorder. I'm a non Christian - like most
Christians. If God chose George Bush..of all the world's people,
how good is God?! You can't talk directly to God. That's bad.
First you've got to talk to a priest. Then Mary. Then Jesus...
It's like going to the DMV. If you have a few hundred followers,
and you let some of them molest children, they call you a
Cult Leader; if you have a billion, they call you Pope.
There's a phrase we live by in America: "In God We Trust"
It's just where Jesus would want it...on our money!"

John Malkovich

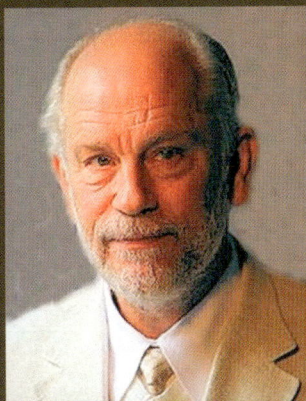

Born 1953 in Christopher, Illinois

American Actor of Croatian Stock

Producer, Director & Fashion Designer

Has Made over 70 Films

"I particularly like Freud

because he was an atheist.

I grew tired of religion

some time not long

after birth.

I believe in humans"

John H Marburger III

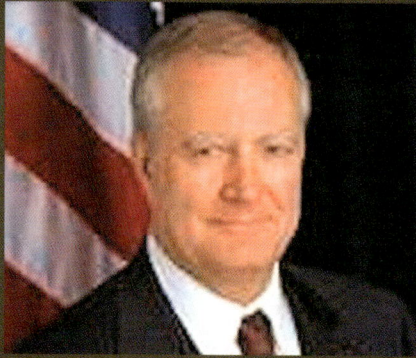

Born 1941 in Staten Island, New York
American Physicist, Science Advisor to
George W Bush's White House
And yet he said;

"Evolution
is the cornerstone of modern biology.
Intelligent Design is not
a scientific theory.
I don't regard Intelligent Design
as a scientific topic!"

Christopher Marlowe

1564-1593 aged 29

Born in Canterbury, Kent

English Dramatist and Poet

He was Just 2 Months Older Than

His Rival, William Shakespeare

Arrested, it is believed, as a Heretic

for Blasphemy, and He was Stabbed to

Death Ten Days Later in a Tavern Fight.

Remembered for "Hero and Leander"

"Dr Faustus", "Tamburlaine" etc

"I count religion but a childish toy,
and hold there is no sin but ignorance.
Religion hides many mischiefs
from suspicion"

Karl Marx

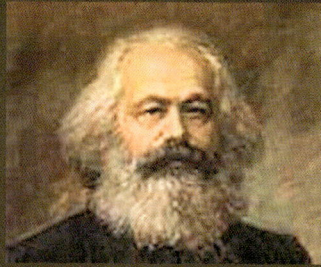

1818-1883 aged 65

Born in Trier, Prussia

Revolutionary Communist

German Philosopher, Socialist,

Political Economist and Theorist

"Religion is the sigh of the oppressed
creature, the heart of a heartless world,
and it is the soul of soulless conditions.
It is the opium of the people.

The theist and the scientist
are rival interpreters of nature,
the one retreats
as the other advances"

Jackie Mason

Born 1936 in Sheboygan, Wisconsin

Brought up in Manhattan, New York

Stand-Up Comedian

Ex-Rabbi !

"Life has no meaning beyond this reality.

I see life as a dance. Does a dance

have to have a meaning?

You're dancing because you enjoy it.

If God exists, he's an idiot.

That's why I don't believe in any God.

Because if that's how he behaves,

I don't want to know such a person"

Geoff Mather

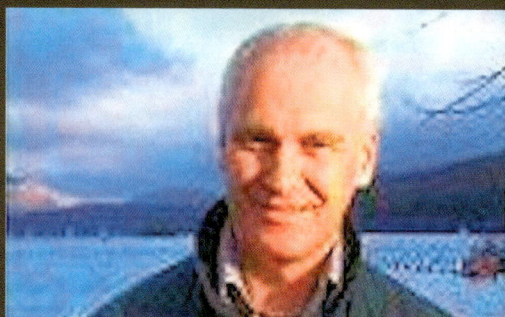

'To say that
atheism
requires faith,
is as dim-witted as saying that
disbelief in pixies or leprechauns
takes faith.
Even if Einstein himself told me
there was an elf on my shoulder,
I would still ask for proof,
and I wouldn't be wrong to ask"

Dave Matthews

Born 1967 in Johannesburg

South Africa

Grew up in New York State

South African Musician

Singer & Songwriter With

The Dave Matthews Band

Actor and Agnostic.

"If there is a God, a caring God,
then we have to figure he's done an
extraordinary job of making
a very cruel world"

W Somerset Maugham

1874-1965 aged 91

Born in Paris, France
English Playwright, Novelist
and World Traveler.
"Religion is a conspiracy of priests
to gain control over people.
There are two good things in life -
freedom of thought and freedom of action.
I cannot believe in a God
that has neither humour nor common sense.
If forty million people say a foolish thing
it does not become a wise one.
There is one thing about which I am certain,
and that is that there is very little about which
one can be certain.
The answer is plain, but it is so unpalatable
that most men will not face it:
there is no reason for life & life has no meaning.
What mean and cruel things men do for the love of God"

Joseph McCabe

1867-1955 aged 88

Born in Macclesfield, Cheshire

Former Roman Catholic Priest

He Renounced His Faith & Wrote

"From Rome to Rationalism"

Wrote Nearly 250 Atheistic Books

And Gave Thousands of Lectures

"Any body of men who believe in hell

will persecute whenever

they have the power"

John McCarthy

Born 1927 in Boston,

Massachusetts

Computer Pioneer

"An atheist

doesn't have to be

someone who thinks he has

proof that there can't be a god.

He only has to be someone who believes

that the evidence on the god question is

at a similar level to the evidence on

the werewolf question"

Colin McGinn

Born 1950 in West Hartlepool, England
Lecturer in Philosophy at
Oxford, Rutgers and Miami Universities

"I don't think the belief in God
has very much to do with
people's moral quality as people.
Faith is believing things
which are not justified by reason.
If it were justified by reason,
it wouldn't be faith"

Sir Ian McKellen

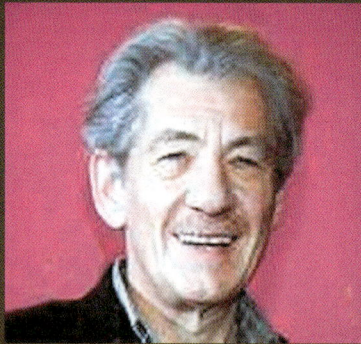

Born 1939 in Burnley, Lancashire

Stage and Film Star

And Activist

"I'm an atheist.
There's a lot about the
Catholic Church I don't approve of,
simply because they don't approve of me.
I've often thought that the Bible should
have a disclaimer at the front saying:
This is fiction
I mean, walking on water!"

Sarah McLachlan

Born 1968 in Halifax, Nova Scotia, Canada

Award Winning Singer, Songwriter and Musician

She has Sold Well Over 40 Million Records

"I'm an agnostic, I don't follow any organized religion"

Here's a song she sang, but didn't write:

Dear God, hope you got the letter and

I pray you can make it better down here.

You're always letting us humans down

The wars you bring, the babes you drown

Those lost at sea and never found

And it's the same the whole world 'round

The hurt I see helps to compound

The Father, Son and Holy Ghost

Is just somebody's unholy hoax

If there's one thing I don't believe in

It's you, dear God

Alexander McQueen

1969-2010 aged 41

Born in Lewisham, London

International Fashion Designer

His clients Include

Mikhail Gorbachev

and Prince Charles

"I'm an atheist and

an anti-royalist!"

And Yet His Designer Made

Kate Middleton's Wedding Dress!

Margaret Mead

1901-1978 aged 77

Born in Philadelphia, Pennsylvania
American Cultural Anthropologist

"Never doubt that a small group of caring,
thoughtful people can change the world.
Indeed, it is the only thing that ever has.
It is an open question whether any behavior
based on fear of eternal punishment can be
regarded as ethical, or should be
regarded as merely cowardly.
Instead of being presented with stereotypes of
age, sex, color, class or religion, children must have
the opportunity to learn that within each range,
some people are loathsome, and some are delightful.
Children must be taught how to think, not what to think.
We won't have a society, if we destroy the environment.
We have nowhere else to go. This is all we have.
Always remember that you are unique,
like everybody else"

Wilhelm Meinhold

1797-1851 aged 54

Born in Netzelkow, Pommern, Germany
A Pastor's Son, He was a Priest, Poet,
Playwright, Author, Novelist & Hymnist
"Christ's transfiguration
and ascension may be compared to the
heathen glorification of
such heroes as Hercules.
While the story of the descent into Hades
is modeled after such narratives
as those describing the visit of
Hercules and Theseus
to the lower world"

H L Mencken

1880~1956 aged 76

Born in Baltimore, Maryland

Journalist, Essayist, Satirist, Editor and Social Critic

"Faith
may be defined as an illogical belief..in the improbable.
I believe that religion has been a curse to mankind...
by the damage it has done to clear and honest thinking.
I believe in the complete freedom of thought and speech.
I believe that it is better to tell the truth than to lie.
I believe that it is better to be free than to be a slave.
I believe that it is better to know than to be
ignorant. The most curious social convention
is that religious opinions should be respected.
We must respect the other fellow's religion..only to
the extent that we respect his theory that his wife
is beautiful and his kids are smart"

James Michener

1907–1997 aged 90

Born in Doylestown, Pennsylvania

American Novelist

More Than 40 Titles including

Tales of the South Pacific, etc

Pulitzer Prize for Fiction in 1948

"Religious hatreds
ought not to be propagated at all,
but certainly not on a
tax-exempt basis!"

John Stuart Mill

1806-1873 aged 67

Born in London, England

Philosopher, Civil Servant

and Member of Parliament

Of Liberal Political Philosophy

"A being who can create a race of men...
foredoomed to be sinners, and then punish
them for being what he has made them, may be
omnipotent..but he is not what the English
language has always intended by the adjective
holy.

Modern morality is derived from Greek and
Roman sources, not from Christianity"

Dennis Miller

Born 1953 in Pittsburgh, Pennsylvania

American Stand-Up Comedian

Actor, Political Commentator

TV and Radio Personality

"Me Born Again?

No I'm not.

Excuse me

for not getting it right

the first time!"

These televangelists say they don't favor any

particular denomination, but I think we've

all seen their eyes light up at

tens and twenties!"

Sir Jonathan Miller

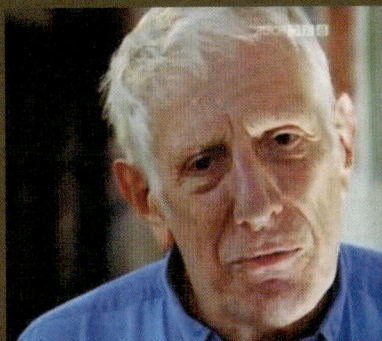

Born 1934 in St John's Wood, London

English Theatre and Opera Director

Author, TV Presenter, Sculptor

Humorist and Atheist

Trained as a Physician

"My father was Jewish

my mother wasn't.

I'm Jew-ish!

In some awful, strange

paradoxical way,

atheists tend to take

religion more seriously

than the practitioners"

Spike Milligan

1918-2002 aged 84

Born in Ahmednagar, India

Irish Comedian, Writer, Musician,

Poet, Playwright, Soldier and Actor

Famous For His "Goon Show" on Radio and TV

"And God said "Let there be light" and there was light, but the Electricity Board said he'd have to wait 'til Thursday to be connected.
Priest: What do we have first to do, so that our sins will be forgiven? Sir, we have to sin.
Adam was the luckiest man in the World - no competition! "Madam, I'm Adam"
How long was I in church? Five foot eleven.
I'm not afraid of dying, I just don't want to be there when it happens. I'd like to go to heaven, but if Jeffrey Archer's there, I'd rather go to Lewisham"

A A Milne

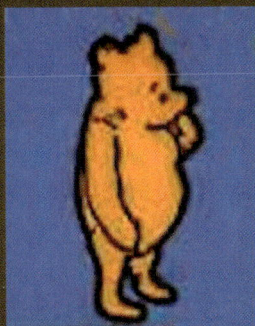

1882-1956 aged 74

Born in Hampstead, London

English Author, Poet & Playwright

Best Known for "Winnie-the-Pooh"

"The Old Testament is responsible
for more atheism, agnosticism and
disbelief than any book ever written;
it has emptied more churches than
all the counterattractions of
cinema, motor bicycle
and golf course"

Ashley Montagu

1905-1999 aged 94

Born in London, England

British-American

Anthropologist and Humanist

"The Good Book -
one of the most remarkable
euphemisms ever coined.
Science has proof
without certainty.
Creationists have certainty
without proof"

Michel de Montaigne

Chateau de Montaigne   1533-1592 aged 57

Born in Saint-Michel-de-Montaigne, France

Influential Writer and Statesman

"Religion is made to eradicate vices,
instead, it encourages them,
covers them & nurtures them.

Oh senseless man, who cannot possibly make a worm,
and yet will make Gods by the dozens.

Men of simple understanding, little inquisitive
and little instructed, make good Christians.

Nothing is so firmly believed as that which we least
know. It is setting a high value upon our opinions,
to roast men alive on account of them.

How many things served us but yesterday as
articles of faith, which today we deem but fables?

The only thing that is certain -
is nothing is certain"

Michael Moore

Born 1954 in Flint, Michigan

American Filmmaker

Author & Liberal Political Activist

"Fahrenheit 9/11" "Sicko" and

"Capitalism, A Love Story" etc

"There's a gullible side to the
American people.
They can be easily misled.
Religion is the best device
used to mislead them"

Desmond Morris

Born 1928 in Purton, Wiltshire

British Zoologist, Anthropologist

Ethnologist, Surrealist Painter

TV Presenter and Author of

"The Naked Ape" etc

"There have been many arguments

about the location of the human soul.

Could it be in the heart, in the head,

or perhaps diffused throughout the whole body.

The answer, it seems to me as a zoologist,

is obvious enough: a man's soul is located

in his testicles; a woman's in her ovaries.

For it is here that we find the truly immortal

elements in our constitution—our genes"

Bill Moyers

Born 1934 in Hugo, Oklahoma

Journalist and Commentator

Has received Over 30 Emmys, etc

Was President Johnson's White House Press Secretary.

"The ruins were still smoldering when Pat Robertson and Jerry Falwell proclaimed on TV that the terrorist 9/11 attacks were God's punishment of a corrupted America...that the government had adopted the agenda of the pagans, and the abortionists, and the feminists, and the gays and lesbians.   Just as God had sent the Great Flood to wipe out a corrupted world, now God almighty is lifting his protection from us. Critics said that such comments were deranged. But many millions of Christian fundamentalists and conservatives didn't think so. They thought Robertson and Falwell were being perfectly consistent with the logic of the Bible as they read it. Not many people at the time seemed to notice that Osama bin Laden had also been reading <u>his</u> sacred book, closely and literally"

Daniel Patrick Moynihan

1927-2003 aged 76

Born in Tulsa, Oklahoma

Brought up in New York City

American Democratic Politician

and Sociologist. Was also

US Ambassador

to India and the United Nations

"Everyone is entitled
to his own opinion
but not his own facts"

The Prophet Muhammad

570-632 aged 62

Born in Mecca. Saudi Arabia

Founder of Islam

Messenger and Prophet of Allah

Shepherd, Merchant, Philosopher, Orator

Diplomat, Legislator, Reformer & General.

Allah's Instructions to Muhammad
in the Qur'an:

"Slay the idolaters wherever ye find them…"

"Fight those who believe not in Allah….

nor acknowledge the religion of Truth…"

"Smite ye above their necks

and smite all their finger-tips off them"

"O Prophet! Exhort the believers to fight…"

(VERY PEACE LOVING!)

Benito Mussolini, "Il Duce"

1883-1945 aged 62

Born in Dovia di Predappo, Italy

Italy's Fascist Dictator

10 June 1940, Declared War on France & Britain

28 April 1945, was Executed by Italian Patriots

His mother was a Devout Catholic, and He Decided to Work with the Catholic Church. He Had a Catholic Wedding & had His Children Baptized. He Closed Down Many Wine Shops and Night Clubs, and Made Swearing in Public a Crime. He Wanted Contraception and Divorce Banned. The Catholic Church was given 30 Million Lira in 1929 and 109 Acres in Rome to Create The Vatican State. The Pope was Also Given as a Country Retreat, Castel Gondolfo.
The Roman Catholic Faith was the State religion.

"We have buried the putrid corpse of liberty"

Vladimir Nabokov

1899-1977 aged 78
Born in St Petersburg, Russia.
Multilingual Russian-American
Novelist. His Family Spoke Russian,
English and French. In Fact, He Could
Read and Write English Before Russian.
In 1940, his Family Moved to Manhattan.
He's Most Famous for "Lolita" in 1955
"Common sense tells us that our
existence is but a brief crack of
light between two eternities
of darkness"

Pandit Nehru

1889-1964 aged 75

Born in Allahabad, India

First, Prime Minister, from 1947 to 1964.

A Leading Figure in India's Independence Movement

"I want nothing to do with any religion concerned with keeping the masses satisfied to live in hunger, filth and ignorance. I want nothing to do with any religion which does not teach people that they are capable of becoming happier and more civilized on this earth, capable of becoming a true man, master of his fate and captain of his soul. To attain this, I would put priests to work, and turn the temples into schools. The spectacle of what is called religion..in India and elsewhere, has filled us with horror, and I have frequently condemned it, and wished to make a clean sweep of it"

Sir Isaac Newton

1643-1727 aged 84

Born in Woolsthorpe Manor, Lincolnshire

English Physicist, Alchemist, Theologian

Astronomer, Philosopher & Mathematician

"I know not how I seem to others,
but to myself I am but a small child
wandering upon the vast shores of knowledge,
every now and then, finding a small bright
pebble to content myself with,
while the vast ocean of
undiscovered truth
lay before me"

"Nature and nature's law lay hid in night,
God said 'Let Newton be' and all was light"
- Alexander Pope

Jack Nicholson

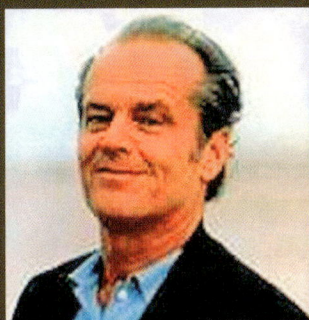

Born 1937 in New York City

Award Winning Film Actor

Producer, Director & Writer

"I resist all

established religions.

My religion is to

live in the now.

I'm incapable of believing

in anything supernatural"

Friedrich Nietzsch

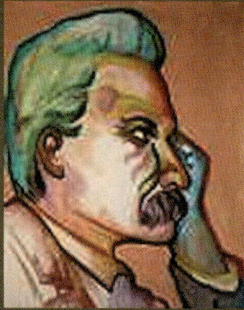

1844~1900 aged 56
Born Near Leipzig, Prussian Saxony
German Philosopher, Poet & Philologist
His Father was a Lutheran Pastor

*"The Christian resolve to find the world
evil and ugly, has made the world evil and ugly.
Wherever on earth the religious neurosis has appeared,
we find it tied to three dangerous dietary demands:*
solitude, fasting and sexual abstinence.
*So long as the priest, that professional negator, slanderer
and poisoner of life, is regarded as a superior type of
human being, there cannot be any answer to the
question: What is Truth?*
*Whatever the theologian regards as true must be false:
there you have almost a criterion of truth.
Faith means not wanting to know what is true"*

Mark A Noll

Born in 1946

Evangelical Christian

Professor of History of American
Christianity

"Early America
does not deserve to be considered
uniquely, distinctly or even
predominantly
Christian..
There is no lost Golden Age
to which American Christians
may return"

Charles Eliot Norton

1827-1908 at 81

Born in Cambridge, Massachusetts

A Leading American Author

Militant Idealist, Liberal Activist

Social Critic & Progressive

Social Reformer

Described as the

Most Cultivated Man in the US

"The loss of religious faith among the most

civilized portion of the race is

a step from childishness

toward maturity"

Sean O'Casey

1880-1964 at 84

Born in Dublin, Ireland

Playwright, Memoirist & Socialist

Most Famous for
"Juno and the Paycock"

"What time has been wasted during man's destiny in the struggle to decide what man's next world will be like! The keener the effort to find out, the less he knew about the one he lived in"

Madalyn Murray O'Hair

1919-1995 aged 76

Born in Pittsburgh, Pennsylvania

American Atheist Activist

Founder of American Atheists

She won a Supreme Court Ruling Ending Government

Sponsored Prayers in American Public Schools.

In 1995 She was Kidnapped and Murdered

"Religion has ever been anti-human, anti-woman, anti-life, anti-peace, anti-reason, and anti-science. The god idea has been detrimental, not only to mankind, but to the earth. It is time now for reason, education and science to take over. Intolerance has always been one of the cornerstones of Christianity - the glorious heritage of the Inquisition. To explain the unknown by the known, is a logical procedure; to explain the known by the unknown, is a form of theological lunacy. The thing I'm most proud of is that people can say 'I'm an atheist' in the US today, without being called a Communist Atheist or an Atheist Communist. I separated the two words".

Eugene O'Neill

1888-1953 aged 65

Born in Manhattan, New York

Classic American Playwright

Nobel Laureate in Literature

"Long Day's Journey into Night"

"Mourning Becomes Electra"

"Desire under the Elms"

'The Iceman Cometh"

"I never took much stock
in the truck them sky-pilots preach.
When men make Gods, there is no God!
Obsessed by a fairy tale, we spend our lives
searching for a magic door, and a
lost kingdom of peace"

Bill O'Reilly

Born 1949 in Manhattan, New York
American Right-Wing Fox TV Host
Catholic, Conservative Commentator
Author and Columnist
"Anti-religious zealots in America, have powerful
allies in the media and succeeded in intimidating
their opposition, using vile tactics. Twenty years
ago, religion was not under siege in America. Now it
is, big time, and only you, the folks, can stop it. The
rise and fall of the tides is a mystery. Humans are
clueless on what causes the tides. God causes the
tides, not the moon. You want to have two guys
making out in front of your 4 year old? It's OK with
atheists. A guy smoking a joint, blowing
smoke into a little kid's face?
OK with them. And I'm not exaggerating here. This
is exactly what the secular movement stands for"

George Orwell

1903-1950 aged 47

Born in Motihari, India

English Author, Journalist and Poet

Most Famous for his Novel Published in 1949

"Nineteen Eighty-Four"

"One defeats a fanatic, precisely by not
being a fanatic oneself,
but on the contrary, by using
one's intelligence.
If liberty means anything at all,
it means the right to tell people
what they do not want to hear"

John Osborne

1929-1994 aged 65

Born in London

English Playwright, Screenwriter

Actor and Critic of the Establishment

Most Famous for his Ground-Breaking Play

"Look Back in Anger" and for his Screenplay

of Tony Richardson's Film "Tom Jones"

"Here we are, we're alone in the universe, there's
no God. It just seems that it all began by
something as simple as sunlight striking on a
piece of rock. We've only got ourselves.
Somehow we've got to make a go of it.
We've only ourselves. Don't be afraid
of being emotional. You won't die of it"

Peter O'Toole

As Lawrence of Arabia

Born 1932 in Connemara, Ireland

Award Winning

Irish Stage and Film Star

"When did I realize I was God?
Well, I was praying,
and I suddenly realized I was
talking to myself!"

Robert Owen

1771-1858 aged 87

Born in Newtown, Wales

Welsh Social Reformer & Philanthropist

One of the Founders of Socialism

Also of Infant Childcare

"Finding that no religion is based on facts,
and cannot therefore be true, I began to reflect
what must be the condition of mankind
trained from infancy to believe in errors.
All religions are based on the same ridiculous
imagination that make a man a weak,
imbecilic animal, a furious bigot and fanatic;
or a miserable hypocrite"

Camille Paglia

Born 1947 in Endicott, New York

Dissident Feminist, Controversial Columnist

Witty Conversationalist, TV Personality

Critic, Author and Bête Noir of Feminists

As a Fellow Feminist Commented;

the 'g' is Silent—

the Only Thing About Her That Is!

She Describes Herself as a

Feminist Bisexual Egomaniac!

"As an atheist,

I acknowledge that religion may be socially

necessary as an ethical counterweight to natural

human ferocity. The primitive marauding impulse

can emerge very swiftly in the alienated young.

Although I'm an atheist who believes only in great

nature, I recognize the spiritual richness and

grandeur of the Roman Catholicism

in which I was raised.

Thomas Paine

1737-1809 aged 72

Born in Thetford, England

American Author and Revolutionary Leader.

One of the Founding Fathers

Wrote "Common Sense" & "The Age of Reason"

In England, Sellers of the Book were Jailed for Blasphemy

"The Bible is such a book of lies and contradictions, there is no knowing which part to believe, or whether any.

It is a history of bad times and bad men. There are but a few good men in the whole book. It is a history of wickedness that has served to corrupt and brutalize mankind; and for my part, I sincerely detest it, as I detest everything that is cruel. All the tales of miracles with which the Old Testament and New Testament are filled, are fit only for imposters to preach and fools to believe. Of all the tyrannies that afflict mankind, tyranny in religion is the worst. Every other species of tyranny is limited to the world we live in, but this attempts a stride beyond the grave and seeks to pursue us into eternity"

"I do not believe in the creed professed by the Jewish church, the Roman, the Greek, the Turkish, the Protestant church nor by any church that I know of. My own mind is my church.

Thomas Paine...continued

All national institutions of churches, whether Jewish, Christian or Turkish, appear to me no other than human inventions, set up to terrify and enslave mankind, and monopolize power and <u>profit</u>. What is it the Bible teaches us? - raping, cruelty, and murder. What is it the New Testament teaches us? - to believe that the Almighty committed debauchery with a woman engaged to be married, and the belief of this debauchery is called faith. Whenever we read the obscene stories, the voluptuous debaucheries, the cruel and torturous executions, the unrelenting vindictiveness with which more than half the Bible is filled, it would be more consistent that we call it the word of a demon, than the word of God. The continually progressive change to which the meanings of words is subject, the errors to which translations are subject, the mistakes of copyists and printers, the possibility of willful alteration, are evidences that human language, whether in speech or in print, cannot be the vehicle of the Word of God. The most detestable wickedness, the most horrid cruelties, and the greatest miseries that have afflicted the human race, have had their origin in this thing called revelation, or revealed religion. The world is my country, all mankind are my brethren, and to do good is my religion. I believe in the equality of man; and I believe that religious duties consist in doing justice, loving mercy & endeavoring to make our fellow-creatures happy.

Sarah Palin

Born 1964 in Sandpoint, Idaho

Ex-Beauty Queen, Ex-Mayor of Wasilla, Alaska

Ex-Governor of Alaska, Until she Quit.

Was John McCain's Surprising Choice for

Potential Vice-President, in the 2008 Election.

A Republican, She's a Tea Party Favorite

"It would be wise for us to start seeking some divine intervention again in this country, so that we can be safe and secure and prosperous again. I think we should keep this clean, keep it simple, go back to what our founders and our founding documents meant. They're quite clear, that we would create law, based on the God of the Bible and the Ten Commandments"

GEORGE WASHINGTON:

"THE UNITED STATES OF AMERICA
SHOULD HAVE A FOUNDATION FREE FROM
THE INFLUENCE OF THE CLERGY"

JOHN ADAMS: "THE UNITED STATES OF AMERICA IS IN
NO SENSE FOUNDED ON THE CHRISTIAN RELIGION"

Olof Palme

1927-1986 aged 59

Born in Stockholm, Sweden

Leader of the Swedish Social Democratic Party

Was 2 term Prime Minister until His Assassination.

It is Suspected that his Harsh Criticism of

South African Apartheid and

Prime Ministers John Vorster and P W Botha

May Have Lead to His Being Killed.

Palme is Said to be Partly Responsible for the

Wide-Spread Disbelief in Sweden.

He had Conflicts with the Church of Sweden,

Because he Wished to Separate it Completely from

the State. He Said

"Human beings will find a balanced situation

when they do good things, not because God says it,

but because they feel like doing them"

Dorothy Parker

1893-1967 aged 73

Born in Long Branch, New Jersey

American Poet, Satirist, Wit & Wisecracker

Writer for New Yorker, Screenwriter and Critic

Founding Member of the Algonquin Round Table

"I went to a convent school in New York
and was fired finally for my insistence that the
Immaculate Conception
was a spontaneous combustion.
Well, Evangelist Aimee Semple McPherson
has written a book...It may be that this
autobiography is set down in sincerity,
frankness and simple effort.
It may be, too, that the Statue of Liberty
is situated in Lake Ontario"

Matthew Parris

Born 1949 in Johannesburg,
South Africa
British Journalist & Ex-Conservative
Member of Parliament

"All three of
our major religions in Britain -
Christianity, Islam and Judaism -
have a hateful idea at the very core.
That idea is Exclusion:
the "othering"...of the unredeemed.

Pope Paul III

1468-1549 aged 81

Born in Canino, Italy

Reigned as Pope From 1543 to 1549

"I will, when opportunity presents,
wage relentless war, secretly or openly,
against all Heretics, Protestants and Liberals,
as I am directed to do, and to exterminate them
from the face of the whole earth, and that I will
spare neither sex, age nor condition and that I
will hang, waste , boil, flay, strangle and bury
alive these infamous heretics; rip up the
stomachs and wombs of their women and crush
their infants' heads against the wall, in order to
annihilate forever their execrable race"

CHARMING!

Pope Paul IV

1476-1559 aged 83

Born near Avelino, Italy

Reigned as Pope from 1555 to 1559

He created the Ghetto of Rome

Claiming that God had Condemned

the Jews to Lifelong Slavery.

"If my own father were a heretic,
I would personally gather
the wood to burn him"
APAULING!

Penn and Teller

Penn born 1955 in Greenfield, Mass.
Teller born 1948 Philadelphia, Penn.
(Penn Talks a Lot..Teller Never Tells!)
Broadway and Las Vegas Entertainers
Illusionists, Atheists, Comedians
Magicians, Skeptics and Libertarians

"The characters and events depicted in the
damn bible are fictitious. Any similarity
to actual persons, living or dead, is purely
coincidental. What has been Christianity's
fruits? Superstition, Bigotry and Persecution.
Believing there is no God gives me more room for
belief in family, people, love, truth, beauty,
sex, Jell-o, and all the other things I
can prove, and that make this life
the best life I will ever have"

Joaquin Phoenix

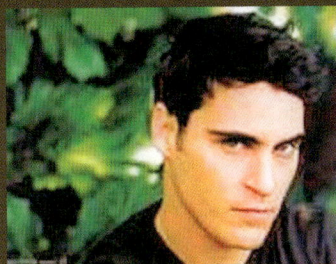

Born 1974 in San Juan

Puerto Rico

Actor, Activist

Director, Producer

Recording & Rap Artist

"I'm not into organized

religion...

To me it's a pretty preposterous

idea"

Emo Philips

Born 1956 in Chicago, Illinois
American Stand-Up Comedian
and Entertainer

"When I was a kid
I used to pray every night
for a new bicycle.
Then I realized that the Lord
doesn't work that way
...so I stole one
and asked him to forgive me"

Pablo Picasso

1881-1973 aged 92

Born in Malaga, Spain

Lived Mostly in France

Revolutionary Spanish Painter

and Sculptor

Co-Founder of the

Cubist Movement

"God is really only another artist.
He invented the giraffe, the elephant,
and the cat.
He has no real style.
He just keeps on trying other things"

Steven Pinker

Born 1954 in Montréal, Canada
Canadian-American Psychologist
Cognitive Scientist, Linguist
and Science Fiction Writer
Harvard Psychology Professor
"For anyone with a persistent intellectual
curiosity, religious explanations are not worth
knowing because they pile equally baffling
enigmas on top of the original ones. What gave God a
mind, free will, knowledge, certainty about right
and wrong? How does he infuse them into a universe
that seems to run just fine according to physical
laws?...And most perplexing, if the world unfolds
according to a wise and merciful plan, why does it
contain so much suffering?
As the Yiddish expression says, If God lived on earth,
people would break his window"

Harold Pinter

1930-2008 aged 78

Born in Hackney, London

English Playwright, Screenwriter

Actor, Activist, Director and Poet

Nobel Prize in Literature in 2005.

In His 50 Year Career He wrote 29 Plays, including

"The Caretaker" & "The Birthday Party" and 27

Screenplays including "The Servant" and

"The French Lieutenant's Woman"

His Religion was Judaism, Then Catholicism

and Finally, Atheism!

"The George W Bush Administration are a bunch of

criminal lunatics. I just don't see how Bush and

Blair can claim to be Christians

and still bomb innocent people"

"There is no flag large enough to cover the shame of

killing innocent people"...Howard Zinn

Robert M Pirsig

Born 1928 in Minneapolis, Minnesota
American Writer & Zen Philosopher

"When one person suffers from a delusion,
it's called insanity. When <u>many</u> people
suffer from a delusion it's called religion.
You are never dedicated to something
you have complete confidence in.
When people are fanatically dedicated to
political or religious faiths, or any other
kind of dogmas or goals, it's always because
these dogmas or goals are in doubt.
No one is fanatically shouting
that the sun is going to rise tomorrow.
They <u>know</u> it's going to rise tomorrow"

Brad Pitt

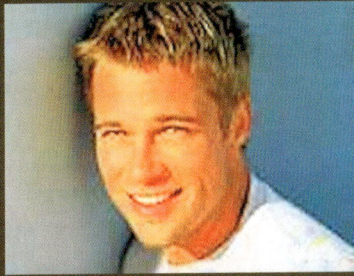

Born 1963 in Shawnee, Oklahoma
Raised Southern Baptist in
Springfield, Missouri

"I'm 20% atheist and 80% agnostic!
I didn't understand this idea of a God who says
'You have to acknowledge me. You have to say I'm
the best, and then I'll give you eternal happiness.
If you won't, then you don't get it.'
It seemed to be about ego. I can't see God
operating from ego, so it made no sense to me.
When I got untethered from the comfort of religion,
it wasn't a loss of faith for me. It was discovery of
self. I had thought that I'm capable enough to
handle any situation. There's peace in
understanding that I have only one life,
here and now, and I'm responsible"

Pope Pius XI

1857 - 1939 aged 81

Born in Desio, Lombardy-Venetia

Austrian Empire

Reigned as Pope from 1922 to 1939

"Mussolini is a wonderful man.

Do you hear me?

A wonderful man"

Pope Pius IX

1792-1878 aged 86

Born in Senigallia, Papal States, Italy
Reigned as Pope from 1846 to 1878

"The aberrations of Darwinism,
a system which is repugnant...to history,
to the tradition of all people, to exact
science, to observed facts, and even to reason
itself, would seem to need no refutation.
But the corruption of this age,
the machinations of the perverse,
the danger of the simple,
demand that such fancies,
altogether absurd though they are, should
- since they borrow the mask of science -
be refuted by true science"

Plato

428 BC-348BC aged 80

Born in Athens

Classical Greek Philosopher

Student of Socrates and Founder of

The Academy in Athens, the First Institution

of Higher Learning in the Western World.

"A certain portion of mankind do not believe at

all in the existence of the gods...Though a man

should be a complete unbeliever in the being of

the gods; if he also has an native uprightness of

temper, such persons will detest evil in men;

their repugnance to wrong, disinclines them to

commit wrongful acts, they shun the

unrighteous, and are drawn to the upright"

Edgar Allan Poe

1809-1849-aged 40   His Cottage in The Bronx, NY

Born in Boston, Massachusetts

Raised an Orphan in Richmond, Virginia

American Author, Poet, Editor & Literary Critic

Famous for his Tales of Mystery and the Macabre

"The pioneers and missionaries
of religion have been the real cause of
more trouble and war than all the other
classes of mankind.   No man who ever lived
knows any more about the hereafter
than you or I; and all religion is simply
evolved out of chicanery, fear, greed,
imagination and poetry"

Ezra Pound

1885-1972 aged 87
Born in Hailey, Idaho
Raised in Pennsylvania
American Expatriate Poet & Critic
Working in London as Editor of Several American
Literary Magazines, He helped Discover
T S Elliott, James Joyce,
Robert Frost and Ernest Hemmingway.
He later Lived and Worked in Paris
and in Rapallo on the Italian Riviera.

"Religion, oh, just another of those numerous
failures from an attempt to popularize art.
Christ, a heroic figure.. not wholly to blame for
the religion that's been foisted on him"

Paula Poundstone

Born 1959 in Huntsville, Alabama
American Stand-Up Comedienne
Well Known on NPR's
"Wait, Wait, Don't Tell Me!" etc
She Has 4 Adopted Children & Lots of Cats.
"I'm totally an asexual atheist human being!
I am not at this time a virgin myself,
but I don't like sex, so I abstain, which would
certainly be at least a cousin to virgin, perhaps
deserving something in an honorary title.
Should I become a beloved hero in my time,
my followers could refer to me as "Viginish".
The idea that I'd get to my bed and there'd be
someone in there with whom I was supposed to
have an activity, is horrifying to me.
The Wages of Sin are Death,
but after they take the taxes out,
it's more like a tired feeling, really!"

Proverbs, 3:5 from the Bible

"Trust in the LORD
with all your heart,
on your own intelligence
rely not"
and
"A simple man believes
anything,
but a prudent man
gives thought to his step"
Proverbs 14:15

Quintus

239 BC–169 BC aged 70
Born in Radian, Calabria, Italy
Roman Writer and Poet
Father of Roman Poetry
"How like us
is that ugly brute, the ape!"

Daniel Radcliff

Born 1989 in Hammersmith, London
English Film & Stage Actor, Cast at Age 11 as
Harry Potter, and from 2001 to 2011
He has Played the Part
in 8 Films in the Series
He Now has Assets of
Over 28 Million Pounds,
Making Him Richer Than
Princes William and Harry!

"I'm an atheist, but I'm very relaxed
about it. I don't preach my atheism,
but I have enormous respect for people
like Richard Dawkins who do.
Yes, I'm an atheist
and am very proud of being Jewish"

Ayn Rand

1905-1982 aged 77
Born in Saint Petersburg, Russia
Russian-American Novelist, Philosopher,
Playwright & Screenwriter
Moved to the US in 1926 and is Most Famous for
"The Fountainhead" "Atlas Shrugged"
and "The Virtue of Selfishness"
"I am an intransigent atheist, but not a militant one.
This means that I am fighting for reason, not <u>against</u>
religion. The Cross is a symbol of torture. I prefer the $
sign-the symbol of free trade, therefore of a free mind.
Religion is a primitive form of philosophy, the attempt to
offer a comprehensive view of reality. If devotion to truth
is the hallmark of morality, then there is no greater,
nobler, more heroic form of devotion than the act of a
man who assumes the responsibility of thinking. Ask
yourself whether the dream of heaven and greatness
should be waiting for us in our graves - or whether it
should be ours here and now and on this Earth.
The Founding Fathers were neither passive,
death-worshipping mystics nor mindless,
power-seeking looters...they were thinkers,
who were also men of action"

James Randi

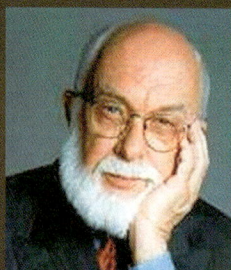

Born 1928 in Toronto, Canada
Stage Magician and Scientific Skeptic.
Challenger of Paranormal Claims
and Pseudoscience

"I hereby state my opinion that the notion of
a god is a superstition, and that there is no
evidence for the existence of any god or gods.
Further, devils, demons, angels and saints
are myths; there is no life after death,
no heaven or hell; the Pope is a dangerous,
bigoted, medieval dinosaur...I accuse the
Christian god of murder for allowing the
Holocaust to take place..and I condemn..
this mythical deity for encouraging
racial prejudice and commanding
the degradation of women"

Joseph Ratzinger
Pope Benedict XV

Born 1927 in Markti, Bavaria, Germany
265th Pope as from 2005
Previously Archbishop of Munich During
the Height of the Sexual Abuse Scandals
"The Church at the time was much more
faithful to reason than Galileo himself,
and also took into consideration the ethical
and social consequences of Galileo's doctrine.
Its verdict against Galileo was
rational and just."
"Show me just what Muhammad brought that
was new, and there you will find things only
evil and inhuman, such as his command to
spread by the sword, the faith he preached"
WHAT ABOUT THE CRUSADES
AND THE INQUISITION?

Jonathan Rauch

Born 1960 in Phoenix, Arizona
American Author, Journalist
Activist and Social Critic

"In a liberal society,

to claim that you are above error,

is the height of

irresponsibility"

GEORGE W BUSH, PLEASE NOTE!

William Winwood Reade

1838-1875 aged 37

Born in Perthshire, Scotland
British Historian, Philosopher & Explorer

"There is no study so saddening, and so sublime,
as that of the early religions of mankind..
At first men enjoyed the blessings of nature as children do,
without inquiring into the causes. It was sufficient for them
that the earth gave them herbs, that trees bore them fruit,
that the stream quenched their thirst. They were happy..And
then a system of theology arose amongst them. They taught
each other that the sun, and the earth, the moon, and the stars
were moved and illumined by a Great Soul which was the
source of all life, which caused the birds to sing, the brooks to
murmur, and the sea to heave. To cultivate the intellect is a
religious duty; and when this truth is recognized by men, the
religion that teaches that the intellect should be distrusted,
and that it should be subservient to faith, will inevitably
fall. One fact must be familiar to all those who have
experience of human nature - a sincerely religious
man is often an exceedingly bad man"

Ronald Reagan

1911-2004 aged 93
Born in Tampico, Illinois
40th President of the United States
From 1981 to 1989
Began His Career as a Radio Broadcaster
Then Became a Film and TV Actor
Starred in Over 50 Films
President of the Screen Actors Guild
A Democrat From 1932,
He Switched to Republican in 1962
Was Governor of California 1967 to 1972
After Trying in 1968 and 1976, He Became
United States President in 1981 to 1989
"For the first time ever, everything is in place
for the Battle of Armageddon
and the second coming of Christ"

Ron Reagan

Born 1958 in Los Angeles, California
Son of President Ronald Reagan
Radio Talk Show Host
Liberal and Progressive, Despite his Father
Being a Conservative, Republican Icon.
He Married Doria, a Clinical Psychiatrist in 1980
and They Live in Seattle, Washington.
"My father was a deeply religious man, but he
never made the fatal mistake so many
politicians make, of wearing his religion on
his sleeve to gain political advantage.
I'm an atheist. You know Polls all say that
people won't elect an atheist.
People who believe they are acting with the
mandate of God, who see others who don't
share their beliefs as inferior in the eyes of god
...make dangerous leaders, like Osama bin Laden"

Christopher Reeve

1952-2004 aged 52
Born in New York City
American Actor, Film Director
Producer, Screenwriter and Author
He Made a Notable "Superman".
In 1995, at 43, he was Thrown from His
Horse In a Competition in Virginia and
was Paralyzed for the Rest of his Life.
His brother Ben said: "We are devout
atheists. Christopher thought praying
would be hypocritical; if He didn't pray
before his accident, why pray now?"
Christopher said:"Even though I don't
personally believe in the Lord,
I try to behave as though
He was watching"

Rick Reynolds

Born 1951 in Wood Village, Oregon
Comedian, Actor and Writer
Known for His One Man Shows.
"As far as I can tell
from studying the scriptures,
all you do in heaven is pretty much
just sit around all day and praise the Lord.
I don't know about you,
but I think that after the first,
oh, I don't know, 50 million years of that
I'd start to get a bit bored!"

Joan Rivers

1933-2014 aged 81
Born in Brooklyn, New York City
Emmy Award-Winning Comedienne

A great wit who could make a joke
out of ANYTHING!

"Can we Talk?"
"Grow up America!"
"Religion can be boring,
like housework...you clean your
house and six months later
you have to clean it again!"

Oral Roberts

1918- 2009 aged 91
Born in Ada, Oklahoma
Pentecostal Televangelist in Tulsa, Oklahoma
His Ministry Reached Millions
Worldwide Over Six Decades
One Fan Donated $70 Million!
He Preached Prosperity...
and Practiced What He Preached!
He Told His Audience that God Told Him He Must
Raise $8 Million, or God would "take him home"
Employees Alleged He Spent Ministry Funds
on Clothes, Jewelry and Private Jet Travel.

"Men ..go wild -and then when it's perverted,
and when it becomes homosexual it's not only wild,
it's insane! And the heat becomes so intense, the
sexual heat becomes so intense..they die, they die."
It turned out his son and grandson
were both gay!

Pat Robertson

Born 1930 in Lexington, Virginia

Media Mogul & Televangelist of the Conservative Christian Far Right. Businessman & Ex-Baptist Minister. Host of The 700 Club Daily TV Program Shown Worldwide in 180 Countries in 71 Languages Through His Christian Broadcasting Network. He's thought to be worth as much as a billion dollars.

"If Christians work together, they can succeed in taking back control of the institutions that have been taken from them over the past 70 years. Expect confrontations ..unpleasant..at times bloody. God's people will emerge victorious. Feminism is not about equal rights for women, it's about a socialist, anti-family political movement that encourages women to leave their husbands, kill their children, practice witchcraft, destroy capitalism, and become lesbians. Just like Nazi Germany did to the Jews, so liberal America is now doing to the evangelical Christians. It's no different..more terrible than anything suffered by any minority in history. In Europe, the big word is tolerance. Homosexuals are riding high, Hinduism is Demonic and Islam Satanic. Evolutionists worship atheism, it's their religion"

SAYING ATHEISM IS A RELIGION IS LIKE SAYING NOT BELIEVING IN FAIRIES IS A RELIGION! IN 2011, WHEN NEW YORK STATE LEGALIZED SAME-SEX MARRIAGE, HE WARNED THAT NO NATION HAS EVER SURVIVED, THAT TOLERATED HOMOSEXUALITY!

Gene Roddenberry

1921-1991 aged 70   **Starship Enterprise**

Born in El Paso, Texas & Grew Up in Los Angeles
TV and Screenwriter, Producer and Futurist
Creator of "Star Trek."

"If this is your God, He's not very impressive. He has
so many psychological problems; he's so insecure.
He demands worship every seven days.
We must question the logic of having an all-
knowing, all-powerful God who creates faulty
human beings, and then blames them for his own
mistakes. He's a pretty poor excuse for a Supreme
Being. I condemn false prophets, I condemn the effort
to take away the power of rational decision,
to drain people of their will -
and a hell of a lot of money in the bargain.
Religions vary in their degree of idiocy,
but I reject them all. For most people, religion is
nothing more than a substitute for a
malfunctioning brain"

Ray Romano

Born 1957 in Queens, New York
American Actor, Writer
Stand-up Comedian & Atheist
Famous for His TV Sitcom
"Everybody Loves Raymond"
"I've had people say to me,
look at the sky, the fields,
the ocean, the beautiful sunset.
Isn't that proof positive of God?
I reply, "Following that line of thought,
look at the magnificent rainbows
after a big rainstorm.
Isn't that proof that god is gay?"

Andy Rooney

1919-2011 aged 92

Born in Albany, New York

American TV Personality

Humorist, Journalist

Radio and TV Writer

Famous since 1978 for His Regular

Commentaries on CBS "60 Minutes"

"I'm an atheist...I don't understand religion at all.

I'm sure I'll offend a lot of people by saying this,

but I think it's all nonsense.

Why am I an atheist?

I ask you: Why is anybody not an atheist?

Everyone starts out being an atheist.

No one is born with belief in anything.

Infants are atheists until they are indoctrinated.

I resent anyone pushing their religion on me.

I don't push my atheism on anybody else.

Live and let live.

Not many people practice that

when it comes to religion"

Theodore Roosevelt

1858-1919 aged 60

Born in New York City
26th President of the United States
From 1901 to 1909
Asthmatic, Politician, Soldier,
Explorer, Hunter and Naturalist.
He Began the Construction of the
Panama Canal and Increased the
National Parks from 5 to 10 and
Protected the Grand Canyon.

"To discriminate against a thoroughly
upright citizen because he belongs to a particular
church, or because, like
Abraham Lincoln, he has not avowed his allegiance
to any church, is an outrage
against that liberty of conscience which is one of the
foundations of American life."
AND YET HE DESCRIBED THOMAS PAINE
AS A FILTHY LITTLE ATHEIST!

Mark Rothko

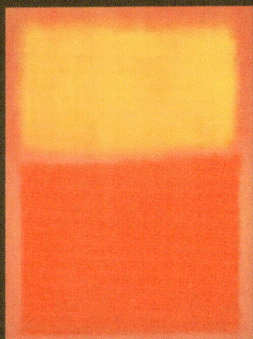

"Orange & Yellow"   1903-1970 aged 66

Born in Dvinks, Russia, Now Latvia

Russian-American

Abstract Impressionist Painter

"I'm not interested
in the relationship
of color or form...
I'm interested in basic human emotions...
tragedy, ecstasy, doom and so on"

His Son Said That his Father Explored
the Idea of Unifying All Religions.
GOOD LUCK WITH THAT IDEA!
His Father Committed Suicide.

Arthur Rubinstein

1887-1982 aged 95
Born in Lodz, Russia, Now Poland
Considered one of the Greatest Pianists
of the 20th Century
He had Perfect Pitch at Two!
He was a Child Prodigy by Four!
"Do I believe in God?
No. You see, what I believe in
is something much greater.
I have found that if you love life,
life lives you back.
I want to enjoy the music
more than the audience.
It's like making love.
The act is always the same,
but each time it's different"

Salman Rushdie KBE

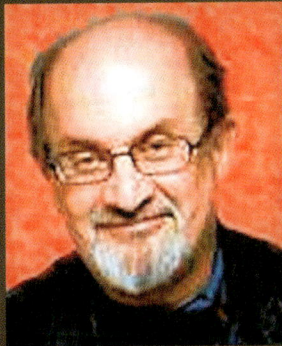

Born 1947 in Bombay, Now Mumbai, India
Muslim Upbringing. Cambridge Graduate
Award Winning Indian-British Novelist and Essayist
Married Four Times. In 1988, His 4th Novel "Satanic Verses"
Produced a Fatwa Against Him by Ayatollah Khomeini.

"God, Satan, Paradise and Hell all vanished one day in my
15th year, when I quite abruptly lost my faith.
I recall it vividly. I was at school in England by then.
The moment of awakening happened, in fact, during
a Latin lesson, and afterwards, to prove my new-found
Atheism, I bought myself a rather tasteless ham sandwich,
and so partook for the first time of the flesh of the swine.
No thunderbolt arrived to strike me down. I remember feeling
that my survival confirmed the correctness of my new position.
I don't think there is a need for an entity like God in my life.
In our darkening world, religion is the poison in the blood...
we go on skating around this issue, speaking of religion in the
fashionable language of 'respect'. What is there to respect in
any of this, or in any of the crimes now being committed
almost daily around the world in religion's dreaded name?
If Woody Allen were a Muslim, he'd be dead by now"

Bertrand Russell

1872-1970 aged 98
Born in Trellech, Wales
Philosopher, Logician, Mathematician, Liberal,
Historian, Social Critic, Socialist and Pacifist.
He was Married Four Times
"My own view on religion is that...I regard it as a disease
born of fear and as a source of untold misery to the
human race. I am as firmly convinced that religions do
harm, as I am that they are untrue. There has been
every kind of cruelty practiced upon all sorts of people in
the name of religion. The infliction of cruelty with a
good conscience is a delight to moralists, that is why they
invented hell. Cruel men believe in a cruel god and use
their belief to excuse their cruelty. Only kindly men
believe in a kindly god, and they would be kindly in
any case. The fundamental cause of trouble in the world
today, is that the stupid are cocksure, while the
intelligent are full of doubt"

Bertrand Russell...continued

"Not to be absolutely certain is, I think, one of the essential things in rationality. One is often told that it is very wrong to attack religion because religion makes men virtuous.
So I'm told; I haven't noticed it.
Religion is based mainly upon fear, fear of the mysterious, fear of defeat, fear of death. Fear is the parent of cruelty, and therefore it is no wonder if cruelty and religion go hand in hand.
As far as I can remember, there is not one word in the Gospels in praise of intelligence.
It is undesirable to believe a proposition when there is no ground whatever for supposing it to be true.
Historically, it is quite doubtful whether Christ ever existed at all, and if he did, we do not know anything about him. We may define "faith" as the firm belief in something for which there is no evidence. Where there is evidence, no one speaks of "faith". We do not speak of faith that two and two are four,
or that the earth is round.
I get letters from people saying, 'God will look after it'. But He never has in the past, I don't know why they they think he will in the future.
What is wanted is not the will to believe, but the will to find out, which is the exact opposite.
The good life is one inspired by love and guided by knowledge"

Marquis de Sade

1740-1814 aged 74
Born in Paris, France
French Aristocrat, Writer
Revolutionary, Playwright.
Famous for His
Libertarian Lifestyle,
His Bisexuality and Blasphemy.

"The idea of God
is the sole wrong for which
I cannot forgive mankind.
There is no God.
The universe runs itself,
and the eternal laws inherent in Nature suffice,
without any first cause or prime mover.
It requires only two things to win credit for a
miracle;
a mountebank and a number of silly women"

Carl Sagan

1934~1996 aged 62
Born in Brooklyn, New York
Astronomer, Astrophysicist, Cosmologist, Author and TV Personality
Famous for His 1981 TV Series "Cosmos" and His Science Fiction Book
"Contact" Filmed With Jody Foster & Matthew McConaughey

"Atheism is more than just the knowledge that gods do not exist,
and that religion is either a mistake or a fraud.
Atheism is an attitude that looks at the world objectively,
fearlessly, always trying to understand all things as a part of
nature. The idea that God is an oversized old white male with a
flowing beard who sits in the sky..is ludicrous. But if by 'God'
one means the set of physical laws that govern the universe, then
clearly there is such a God. This God is emotionally unsatisfying...
it does not make much sense to pray to the law of gravity.
Who is more humble? The scientist who looks at the universe
with an open mind, and accepts whatever the universe has to teach
us ,or somebody who says everything in this book must be considered
the literal truth, and never mind the fallibility of all the human
beings involved? You can't convince a believer of anything; their
belief is not based on evidence, but a deep-seated need to believe.
I would love to believe that when I die I will live again,
that some thinking, feeling, remembering part of me will continue.
But much as I want to believe that, and despite the ancient
and worldwide cultural traditions that assert an afterlife,
I know of nothing to suggest that it is more than just
wishful thinking...there is no reason to deceive ourselves
with pretty stories for which there's no evidence"

Carl Sandburg

1878-1967 aged 89
Born in Galesberg, Illinois
American Writer, Poet,
Soldier, Editor, Folklorist
and Civil Rights Activist
Won 3 Pulitzer Prizes

"To work hard,
to live hard,
to die hard
and then go to hell
after all
would be too
damned hard"

Margaret Sanger

1897-1966 aged 86
Born in Corning, New York
American Sex Educator
and Birth Control Activist
H G Wells Said This About Margaret Sanger:
"Alexander changed a few boundaries
and killed a few men.
Both he and Napoleon were forced into fame by
circumstances outside of themselves and by currents of
the time, but Margaret Sanger made currents and
circumstances. When the history of our civilization is
written, it will be a biological history, and
Margaret Sanger will be its heroine"
She said "Christianity, with some exceptions,
has never explicitly advocated human misery;
it prefers instead to speak of sacrifices in this life,
so that benefits may be garnered in the life to come.
One invests in this life, so to speak, and collects interest
in the next. Fortunately for Christianity,
the dead cannot return for a refund"

Jean Paul Sartre

1905-1980 aged 74
Born in Paris, France
Existentialist Philosopher
Novelist, Political Activist
Playwright, Screenwriter, Biographer
and Literary Critic, Awarded the Nobel
Prize for Literature in 1964, but Refused It.

"Existentialism isn't so atheistic that it wears
itself out showing that God doesn't exist. Rather,
it declares that even if God does exist, that would
change nothing. One day, to while away the time, I
decided to think about God. 'Well' I said, 'he does
not exist'. It was something authentically
self-evident...I settled the question once and for
all at the age of twelve. There is no human nature,
because there is no God to have a conception of it.
Man simply is...Man is nothing else but that which
he makes of himself.
That is the first principle of existentialism"

Olive Schreiner

1855-1920 aged 65 in Wynberg

Born in the Cape, South Africa

South African Author, Intellectual

Anti-War Campaigner

and Political Activist

Friend of Cecil Rhodes

Best known for Her Novel

"The Story Of An African Farm"

"We wretched unbelievers,
we bear our own burdens;
we must say "I myself did it, I.
Not God, not Satan, I myself!"

Charles Schulz

1922-2000 aged 77
Born in Minneapolis, Minnesota
Cartoonist, Writer, Artist
Creator of the "Peanuts" Comic Strip
Which Ran Worldwide From 1950 to 2000
in 21 Languages and Which
Made Him a Billion Dollars!

"Don't worry about the world
coming to an end today.
It's already tomorrow
in Australia!"

Albert Schweitzer

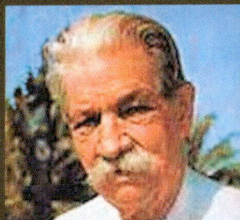

1875-1965 aged 90

Born in Kayserberg, Alsace-Lorraine, Germany, Now France
German Theologian, Philosopher, Physician,
Medical Missionary and Organist.
In 1913 He Founded His Hospital in Lambaréné
in West Central Africa.
He was Awarded the Nobel Peace Prize
in 1952 for his 'Reverence For Life'
He admitted that there isn't a shred of conclusive proof
that Christ ever lived, let alone was the son of God,
that one must therefore accept both on faith.
"There is nothing more negative than the result of the
critical study of life of Jesus. The Jesus of Nazareth who
came forward publicly as the messiah, who preached the
Kingdom of God, who founded the Kingdom of Heaven
upon earth, and died to give his work its final
consecration, never had any existence. He is a figure
designed by rationalism, endowed with life by liberalism,
and clothed by modern theology in an historical garb.
I have always stressed that the destination of
mankind is to become more and more humane.
The ideal of humanity has to be revived"

Dr Seuss

Theodor Seuss Geisel 1904~1991 aged 87
Born in Springfield, Massachusetts
Lived in La Jolla, California
American Writer, Cartoonist & Poet
Best Known for His 46 Children's Books
Like "There's a Wocket in My Pocket" and
"The Cat in the Hat""Green Eggs and Ham"
He was Rejected by 27 Publishers,
Before Selling Millions of Books!
"Be who you are and say what you feel,
because those who mind don't matter,
and those who matter don't mind"
Married Twice, He Had No Children,
He Said "You have 'em
I'll entertain 'em!"

William Shakespeare

Globe Theatre   1564-1616 aged 52   His Birthplace

England's Most Celebrated Playwright and Poet
Acknowledged to be the Finest Dramatist and Poet
in the English Language, Wrote 38 Plays and 154 Sonnets
"The Bard of Stratford-on Avon" But if His Parents
Hadn't Moved, Just Before His Birth, He'd Have Been
"The Bard of Snitterfield"!

"The Devil can cite scripture for his purpose. In religion,
what damned error but some sober brow will bless it, and
approve it with a text, hiding the grossness with fair
ornament?

Methinks sometimes I have no more wit than a Christian.
Modest doubt is call'd the beacon of the wise.
It is the heretic that makes the fire, not she who burns in it.
His worst fault is, he's given to prayer, he is something peevish
that way. Thrust your face into the public street,
to gaze on Christian fools...

Tomorrow, and tomorrow, and tomorrow creeps in this petty
pace from day to day to the last syllable of recorded time; And
all our yesterdays have lighted fools the way to dusty death.
Out, out, brief candle!
Life's but a walking shadow, a poor player that struts and
frets his hour upon the stage and then is heard
no more; it is a tale told by an idiot, full of
sound and fury signifying nothing"

George Bernard Shaw

Born in Dublin, Ireland 1856-1950 aged 94
Irish Playwright, Writer, Critic, Journalist and
Socialist. He Wrote More than 60 Plays. He was
Awarded the Nobel Prize for Literature in 1925
and an Oscar for "Pygmalion" in 1938

"I believe in Michelangelo, Velasquez and Rembrandt;
in the might of design, the mystery of colour,
the redemption of all things by beauty everlasting,
and the message of Art. There is not a single credible established
religion in the world. The early Christian rules of life were not
made to last, because the early Christians did not believe
that the world itself was going to last.
Beware of the man whose God is in the skies,
All great truths begin as blasphemies.
Martyrdom...is the only way in which a man
can become famous without ability.
Emotional excitement reaches men through
tea, tobacco, opium, whiskey and religion.
We have not lost faith, but we have transferred it from
God to the medical profession!"
Why should we take advice on sex from the pope?
if he knows anything about it, he shouldn't!"

Percy Bysshe Shelley

1792-1822 aged 29

Born Near Horsham, Sussex
English Romantic Poet. Expelled From Oxford
For Writing "The Necessity of Atheism" in 1810
Lived His Last Four Years in Italy
"Christianity has equaled Judaism
in the atrocities, and exceeded it in the extent of its
desolation...Millions of men, women, and children
have been killed in battle, butchered in their sleep,
burned to death at festivals ..poisoned, tortured, assassinated
and pillaged in the spirit of the Religion of Peace,
and for the glory of the most merciful God.
And priests dare babble of a God of peace,
Even whilst their hands are red with guiltless blood.
Murdering the while, uprooting every germ of truth,
exterminating, spoiling all, making the earth a slaughter-
house. If he is infinitely good, what reason should we have to
fear him? If he is infinitely wise, why should we have doubts
concerning our future? If he knows all, why warn him of our
needs and fatigue him with our prayers?
If he is everywhere, why erect temples to him?
If ignorance of nature gave birth to gods,
Knowledge of nature is made
for their destruction"

Dave Silverman

Born 1966 in Marblehead,
Massachusetts
President of American Atheists
An Atheist Since He Was A Child
Successful Inventor with 74 Patents

"I have heard many times that
atheists know more about religion
than religious people. Atheism is an
effect of that knowledge - not a lack
of knowledge. I gave a Bible to my
daughter, that's how you make
atheists"

Sarah Silverman

Born 1970 in Bedford, New Hampshire
Comedienne, Writer, Actress
Singer and Musician
Writer and Performer on
"Saturday Night Live"

"Everybody blames the Jews
for killing Christ,
and the Jews try to
pass it off on the Romans.
I'm one of the few people
that believe it was the Blacks"

Homer Simpson

"Born" 1987 in the USA
Cartoon Character
Created by Matt Groening.
He's crude, overweight, incompetent,
clumsy, lazy and ignorant...
but a decent man, devoted to his family.

"I'm not a bad guy! I work hard
and I love my kids.
So why should I spend
half my Sunday
hearing about how
I'm going to hell?
and
Supposing we've chosen the wrong god?
Every time we go to church
we're just making him madder and madder"

Frank Sinatra

and 1915-1998 aged 82
Born in Hoboken, New Jersey
American Singer and Actor
Producer, Director and Conductor
Began His Long Career with
Harry James and Tommy Dorsey.
He Sold Over 150 Million Records!
But Never Learnt To Read Music!
In 1954 He Won An Oscar For
"From Here To Eternity"
He Was Raised Catholic
By His Italian Parents, but...
"When lip service to some mysterious deity
permits bestiality on
Wednesday & absolution on Sunday,
cash me out"

Azura Skye

Born 1981 in Northridge, California
American Film and TV Actress
Began Her Career as a Child Actress

"I wonder who got the shit job of scouring
the planet for the 150,000 species of
butterfly or the 8,800 species of ant they
eventually took on board Noah's Ark.
But at least we got that magical
rainbow for all their trouble"

Socrates

469 BC-399 BC

Classical Greek Athenian
Philosopher
"The unexamined life
is not worth living.
I have not sought during my life
to amass wealth
or to adorn my body,
but I have sought to adorn
my soul with the jewels of
wisdom, patience,
and above all, with
a love of liberty"

Susan Sontag

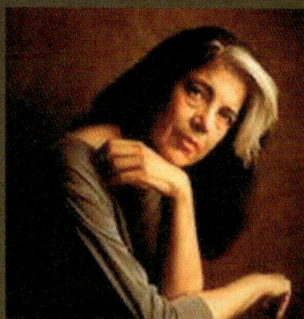

1933-2004 aged 71
Born in New York City
Lived Mostly in Tucson and Paris
American Author, Intellectual
and Political Activist

"Religion
is probably,
after sex,
the second oldest resource
which human beings have
available to them
for blowing their minds"

Mira Sorvino

Born 1967 in Tenafly, New Jersey
Academy Award Winning
American Actress
and Political Activist
Affiliated to Amnesty International
She Graduated from Harvard
Magna Cum Laude, and
Speaks Fluent Mandarin.

"Why does it not say anywhere in the BIBLE
that slavery is <u>wrong</u>?
How is it possible that it is not immoral
to own another person?
Why isn't that one of the Ten Commandments?
'Thou shalt not own another person'
You want to tell me that fornication is
worse than owning someone?"

George Soros

Born 1930 in Budapest, Hungary
Hungarian-American Financier, Businessman
Currency Trader, Investor, Philanthropist
Political Activist, Socialist and Atheist
One of the World's Richest Men, Worth Over $7
Billion, He Supports Liberal Ideals and Causes. In
1947, He Emigrated to England as an Impoverished
Student & Studied at the London School of
Economics and moved to New York City in 1956
He considered America under George W Bush, a
danger to the world. He likened Republicans
generally and the Bush Administration in
particular, to the Nazi and Communist Regimes
'in the sense that they all engage in the politics
of fear' "Once we realize that imperfect
understanding is the human condition, there
is no shame in being wrong, only in failing
to correct our mistakes"

Baruch Spinoza

1632~1677 aged 44

Born in Amsterdam, Holland

Philosopher and Lens Maker

"Philosophy has no end in view save truth:
Faith looks for nothing but obedience and piety.
Those who wish to seek out the cause of miracles,
and to understand the things of nature as
philosophers, and not to stare at them in
astonishment like fools, are soon considered
heretical and impious, and proclaimed as such
by those whom the mob adores as the interpreters
of nature and the gods. For these men know
that once ignorance is put aside, that
wonderment would be taken away, which is
the only means by which their authority is
preserved. I call him free who is led
solely by reason"

John Shelby Spong

Retired Episcopal Bishop of New Jersey

Born 1931 in Charlotte, North Carolina
Liberal Christian 'Nontheist' Theologian
Author and Lecturer, He has Studied at Yale,
Harvard, New York, Edinburgh, Oxford, Cambridge

"I could not believe that anyone who has read this book would be so foolish as to proclaim that the Bible in every literal word was the divinely inspired, inerrant word of God. Have these people simply not read the text? Are they hopelessly misinformed? The God of theism not only is dying, but is probably not revivable. If Christianity depends on a theistic definition of God, then we must face the fact that we are watching this noble religious system enter the rigor mortis of its own death throes...The Bible is an ancient book. There is no other piece of literature written between 1,000BC and 135 AD, which people today still treat as a source of ultimate truth"

Pete Stark

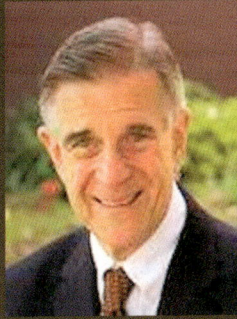

Born 1931 in Milwaukee, Wisconsin
Democratic Congressman for
California's Bay Area Since 1973!
He Got a Bachelor of Science Degree From MIT in 1953
In 1963 He Founded the Security National Bank
in Walnut Creek, Which Now Has
Many Branches in the Bay Area.
He is Very Liberal and Anti-War,
and is the First <u>Openly Atheist</u> Member of Congress.
Hopefully, other Members of Congress Will
Come Out of the Other Closet.

"I am a non-religious person and do not
believe in a supreme being. I'm working to
stop the promotion of narrow religious beliefs
in science, marriage contracts, the military
and the provision of social services"

David Starkey

Born 1945 in Kendal,
Westmoreland
English Historian, Lecturer at
Cambridge and the London School of
Economics, Radio and TV Presenter,
and Gay Rights Activist.
Specialist in the Tudor Era
He has the Reputation for Being the
Rudest Man in Britain
But Isn't!

"I admit freely,
I am a Protestant
Atheist!"

Rod Steiger

1925-2002 aged 77
Born in Westhampton, New York
American Screen Actor in over 100 Films
"Oklahoma!" "On the Waterfront"
and "Jesus of Nazareth" etc
Raised as a Lutheran,
But Lost it Later.

"That's all religion is -
some principle you believe in.
Man has accomplished far more miracles
than the God he invented.
What a tragedy it is,
to invent a God,
and then suffer to
keep him King"

Gertrude Stein

Painting by Picasso

1874-1946 aged 72

Born in Pittsburgh, Pennsylvania

American Writer

and Art Collector

Lived Mostly in Paris

With Alice B Toklas

"There ain't no answer.

There ain't going to be any answer.

There never has been an answer,

That's the answer"

Joel Stein

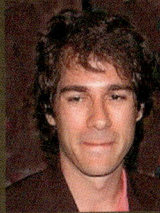

Born 1971 in Edison, New Jersey
BA & MA at Stanford University. Journalist and TV
Personality. Wrote for the Los Angeles Times,
& Since 1997 is a Time Magazine Columnist.

"I had never been to church before. I'd been inside them for weddings, architectural curiosity and once, in college, to hear some guy play the organ so I could hook up with Jenny Hodge. I'm pretty sure God will be cool with that because, as an omnipotent being, he knows how hot she was. But I'd never sat through a service until I went to Austin, Texas, two weeks ago. This mostly has to do with the fact that I'm Jewish but don't believe in God, and sermons don't have nudity, or anything to gamble on. But my college friend Mike had just got ordained as a pastor, so I felt I needed to see his gig. The first thing I noticed, was how dated the songs were, and every so often my eye line was interrupted by an envelope, asking me to donate money. Also, I kept falling asleep. I was surprised how many of the songs and prayers I knew, like the one where I walked through the valley of the shadow of death. In fact, I'd never realized how much of a death cult Christianity is. When we weren't fixating on how awesome Christ's murder was, we were singing about how terrific it was, The whole point of being an atheist is that you don't have to believe that symbolism matters"

John Steinbeck

1902-1968 aged 66
Born in Salinas, California
Nobel Prize Winning
American Novelist
Short Story Writer & War
Correspondent
"Of Mice and Men" "East of Eden"
and "The Grapes of Wrath" etc

"Socialism is just
another form of religion,
and thus
delusional"

Gloria Steinem

Born 1934 in Toledo, Ohio
American Feminist, Journalist
Social and Political Activist
Leader of Women's Liberation

"By the year 2000 (!) we will, I hope,
raise our children to believe in <u>human</u> potential,
not God. However sugarcoated and ambiguous, every
form of authoritarianism must start with a belief
in some group's greater right to power, whether that
right is justified by sex, race, class, religion, or all
four. However far it may expand, the progression
inevitably rests on unequal power, and airtight
roles within the family. It's an incredible con job
when you think of it, to believe something now, in
exchange for life after death. Even corporations
with all their reward systems, don't try to make it
posthumous"

Pope Stephen V

Born in Rome, Italy
Reigned as Pope from 885 to 891

"The Popes, like Jesus, are
conceived by their mothers
through the overshadowing
of the Holy Ghost.
All Popes are a certain species
of man-gods...all powers in
Heaven, as well as on Earth
are given to them"

Howard Stern

Born 1954 in Jackson Heights, New York City
American Radio Personality Known as
The Shock Jock, TV Host, Author and Actor

"Please with the God Talk! I'm sickened
by all religions. Religion has divided people.
I don't think there's any difference between the
pope wearing a large hat and parading around
with a smoking purse, and an African painting
his face white and praying to a rock. I don't
think any religion makes any sense, and I
think people who are into that are really
getting duped, and I don't think Judaism makes
any more sense than Scientology.
But here's a guy, L. Ron Hubbard, who told all
his friends, 'Look, I'm gonna start a religion,
'cause I can't make any money as a science
fiction writer'
I mean, he admitted that publicly!"

Jon Stewart

Born 1962 in New York City
American Political Satirist
Writer, TV Host, Actor
and Stand-Up Comedian
Well Known as the Host of
The Daily Show On TV

"When people say I found God
and that helped me stop drinking,
I say great, but some people stop drinking
without it.

Reason has not been part of religion ever since
two nudists took dietary advice from a talking
snake!"

Peter Stone

1930-2003 aged 73
Born in Los Angeles, California
Award Winning
American Writer for
Stage, TV and Films
"Charade" etc
"When talking about
unicorns, minotaurs,
or compassionate conservatives,
one does not normally have to
<u>prove</u> their non-existence;
the mere lack of any evidence
is sufficient reason not to
believe in any of them"

Andrew Sullivan

Born 1963 in Godstone, Surrey
English-American Author, Journalist, Editor
Conservative Political Commentator,
And Television Personality from an
Irish Roman Catholic Family
Alma Mater: Oxford and Harvard

"The temptation of American and Western culture,
indeed, the very allure of such culture - may well
require a repression all the more brutal, if it is to be
overcome. There is little room in the fundamentalist
psyche for a moderate accommodation. The very
psychological dynamics that lead repressed
homosexuals to be viciously homophobic, or that
entice sexually tempted preachers to inveigh
against immorality, are the same dynamics that
lead vodka-drinking fundamentalists to steer
planes into buildings. It is not designed to achieve
anything, construct anything, or argue anything.
It is a violent acting out of internal conflicts"

Billy Sunday
(William Sonntag)

1862-1935 aged 72
Born in Ames, Iowa
American Baseball Star Player
Who Became the Most Celebrated
and Influential Evangelist,
Holding Mass Conservative Christian
Revival Meetings Around the Country.
When Prohibition was Repealed
He Called for its Reintroduction.

"The rivers of America will run with
blood before they take our holy,
God-inspired Bible from our schools.
America is not a country
for a dissenter to live in"

Jimmy Swaggart

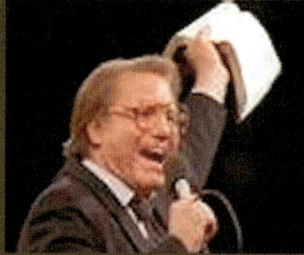

Born 1935 in Ferriday, Louisiana
Pentecostal American Pastor, Since 1975
Preacher, Teacher & Televangelist
In 1988, He was Found to have Solicited a Prostitute
for Sex, Which He Initially Denied, But Later
Admitted and Apologized on TV. He was Defrocked
and Removed From Assemblies of God. Then in 1991,
He was Again Found with a Prostitute. This Time
He Told His Congregation That
"The Lord told me it was none of your business"
"If a Gay ever looks at me like that,
"I'm gonna kill I him, and tell God he died."
"The Supreme Court of
the United States of America
is an institution damned by God Almighty"

His TV Apology

Julia Sweeney

Born 1959 in Spokane, Washington
Award Winning Actress, Author,
Comedienne and Well Known as a Cast
Member of
Saturday Night Live and for Her
Autobiographical Solo Shows Like
"Letting Go of God" - She Grew From
Catholicism to Atheism. When She told Her
Mother That She'd Come to Realize She Was
an Atheist - Her Mother was Horrified:
"I can understand you saying that you
no longer believe in God—but an ATHEIST!"

"I believe the universe can function on its
own without a deity to preside over it"

Jonathan Swift

1667-1745 aged 77   Gulliver

Born in Dublin, Ireland

Satirist, Novelist, Essayist

Poet, Political Pamphleteer

Theologian and Priest, He Became

Dean of St Patrick's Cathedral, Dublin.

Most Famous for "Gulliver's Travels"

"We've got just enough religion
to hate each other,
but not enough religion
to love each other.

It's useless to attempt to
reason a man out of
what he was never
reasoned into"

William H Taft

1857-1930 aged 93
Born in Cincinnati, Ohio
27th President of the United States
From 1909 to 1913, and Later,
10th Chief Justice, From 1921 to 1930,
the Only Person to Serve
in Both Offices.

"I do not believe in the divinity of
Christ, and there are many other
postulates of the orthodox creed to
which I cannot subscribe.
No tendency is quite so strong in
human nature as the desire to lay
down rules of conduct for other people"

James Taylor

Born 1948 in Boston, Massachusetts
Grew Up In Chapel Hill, North Carolina
Five Times Grammy Award Winning
Singer, Songwriter and Guitarist
"You've Got a Friend"
"Carolina On My Mind" etc

"I'm not saying that's not helpful
to think of having a real handle on
the universe, your own personal point
of attachment. But ..I think it's
crazy. But it's an insanity that keeps
us sane. You might call a lot of my
songs 'spirituals for agnostics'.
Maybe you can believe it
if it helps you to sleep"

The Temptations

Formed 1960 in Detroit, Michigan
American Vocal Group with Motown Records
In Their Five Decade Career They've Sold Tens of Millions
of Records. "My Girl" etc

"Listen, people!
Life is a giant, invisible scale
With two sides.
Good and Bad
You and your beliefs
Are the weights.
The things you do each day
Determine the balance.
Your conscience is a flawless
Judge and Jury
The only question
Is what do you want.
I'm tellin' you the natural facts
For what it's worth.
Listen to me, people.
You make your own
Heaven and Hell
Right here on earth"

Mother Teresa

1910-1997 aged 87

Born Agnes Bojaxhiu in Skopje, Macedonia
Albanian Catholic Nun Who Founded
the Missionaries of Charity in India, in 1950.
She Worked With the Very Poor in Calcutta-
(Kolkata) and had 610 Missions in 123 Countries.
She Received the Nobel Peace Prize in 1979.
On the Streets of Calcutta, Where Many Babies are
Born to Starve and Die in Misery, She Said:
"Every baby that takes a breath is another soul to the glory of
God. Suffering? We are all born to suffer. I think it is very
beautiful for the poor to accept their lot, to share it with the
passion of Christ. I think the world is being much helped by the
suffering of the poor people. There are many religions and each
one has its different ways of following God...Jesus is my god.
Jesus is my spouse. Jesus is my life. Jesus is my only love.
Jesus is my all in all. Jesus is my everything." But, sadly
toward the end of her life..."Where is my faith? There is
nothing but darkness...If there be God - Please forgive me.
When I try to raise my thoughts to heaven, there is such
convicting emptiness, that those very thoughts return
like sharp knives and hurt my very soul...How painful is this
unknown pain—I have no Faith. Repulsed, empty,
no faith, no love, no zeal...What do I labor for?
If there be no God, there can be no soul.
If there be no soul then, Jesus, You also are not true"

Randall Terry

Born 1959 in New York City
American Pro-Life Activist Extremist
and Author. (Think Uni-Bomber)

"I don't think Christians should use birth control.
You consummate your marriage as often as you like -
and if you have babies, you have babies. Our goal must be
simple. We must have a Christian nation built on God's
law, on the Ten Commandments. No apologies. The Bible
is the supreme law that all governments must obey. I
want you to just let a wave of intolerance wash over
you. I want you to let a wave of _hatred_ wash over you.
Yes, hate is good. Our goal is a Christian nation..We have
a Biblical duty; we are called by God to conquer this
country. We don't want equal time. We don't want
Pluralism. We want Theocracy. Theocracy means God
rules. I've got a hot flush. God rules. When I, or people
like me are running this country, you'd better flee,
because we will find you, we will try you, and we'll
execute you. I mean every word of it. I will make it part
of my mission to see to it
that they are tried and executed"

Emma Thompson

Born 1959 in London
Award Winning Actress
and Screenwriter
"I'm an atheist.
I regard religion
with fear and suspicion.
It's not enough to say
I don't believe in God.
I actually regard the system
as distressing.
I am offended by some of the things
said in the Bible and the Qur'an,
and I refute them"

Henry Thoreau

Thoreau's Cabin in Walden Woods
1817-1862 aged 44
Born in Concord, Massachusetts
American Author, Poet, Naturalist
Philosopher, Historian, Surveyor & Tax Resister
Best Known for His book "Walden",
His Reflections on Living the Simple Life,
in Natural Surroundings..Walden Woods.

"I do not see why the schoolmaster
should be taxed to support the priest,
and not the priest the schoolmaster.
Do not be too moral!
You may cheat yourself out of much life.
So aim above morality...When you travel to
the Celestial City, carry no letter of
introduction. When you knock,
ask to see God - none of his servants.
Have I made peace with god?
I did not know that we had ever quarreled"

Pat Tillman

1976-2004 aged 27
Born in Freemont, California
American Star Football Player
Who, Following the 9/11 Attacks,
Turned Down a Contract Offer of $3.6 Million
to Enlist in the US Army and Fight in
Afghanistan, only to be killed by 'Friendly Fire'
...Which the Army Initially Denied,
But After Investigation By Congress, the Army
Finally Admitted it. He was an Atheist, in Fact He
Had Some Very Strong Language for a Fellow
Soldier Who Prayed for Him as He was Dying. There
Have Been Rumors That Tillman's Wounds
Suggested Murder, Rather Than Friendly Fire -
He Was Known to be an Atheist, and Highly
Critical of Bush's Iraq War, and was Planning
on His Return to the US to Meet with
Government Critic Noam Chomsky.

The Most Reverend
Bishop Thomas Tobin

Born 1948 in Pittsburgh, Pennsylvania
Bishop of Providence, Rhode Island
Barred Patrick Kennedy from Communion
Due to the Congressman's Support
of Pro-Choice

"Any Catholic in public office,
his first commitment
must be to his <u>faith</u>.
May we be united in faith,
hope and love, as we seek to
live our faith
and share the Good News
of Jesus Christ"

Leo Tolstoy

1828-1910 aged 82

Born in Yasnaya Polyana, Russian
Writer of Novels & Short Stories
Playwright, Essayist & Social Reformer
Most Famous for "War and Peace" and "Anna Karenina"
He Founded 13 Schools in His Area, But was Excommunicated
by the Russian Orthodox Church Which He Called
'An impenetrable forest of stupidity'
"The teaching of the Church is..a crafty and evil lie..a
concoction of gross superstition and witchcraft...The Christian
Churches and Christianity, have nothing in common save the
name; they are utterly hostile opposites. To regard Christ as
God, and to pray to him, are to my mind the greatest possible
sacrilege. Could it be that all this talk of love, goodness, God,
religion, law, justice, and so on, was merely to conceal the
grossest self-interest and cruelty?
Free thinkers are those who are willing to use their minds
without prejudice and without fearing to understand things
that clash with their own customs, privileges, or beliefs.
This state of mind is not common, but it is essential
for right thinking, where it is absent,
discussion is apt to be worse than useless"

Lily Tomlin

Born 1939 in Detroit, Michigan
Award Winning
American Actress
Writer, Comedienne
and Producer

"When you talk to God,
you're praying.
When God talks to you,
you're schizophrenic"

Polly Toynbee

Born 1946 on the Isle of Wight

British Journalist, Columnist, Atheist

Social Democrat, Labour Supporter

Columnist of the Year 2007

With the Guardian Since 1998

President of the British Humanist Association

"Religion is not nice, it kills; it is toxic in the places where people really believe it. It is there in the born-again Christian fundamentalism demanded of every US politician. It drives on the murderous Islamic jihadists. It makes mad the biblical land-grabbing Israeli settlers. It threatens nuclear nemesis between the Hindus and Muslims along the India-Pakistan border. It still hurls pipe bombs on the Ulster streets...the Pope kills millions through his reckless spreading of AIDS. When absolute God-given righteousness beckons, blood flows and women are in chains. The only good religion is a moribund religion. Religion only becomes civilized when it loses all temporal power, in a multicultural secular society. Only when the faithful are weak are they tolerant and peaceful. Only then does religion turn into a gentle talisman of cultural tradition, a mode of meditation with little literal belief in ancient miracles or long dead warlords"

Robert L Trivers

Born 1943

American Evolutionary Biologist
Sociobiologist & Professor of Anthropology
and Biological Sciences at Rutgers
University and Harvard Historian

"The chimpanzee and the human share
about 99.5 percent of their evolutionary
history, yet most human thinkers regard
the chimp as a malformed, irrelevant
oddity, while seeing themselves as
stepping stones to the Almighty"

Harry S Truman

1884-1972 aged 88

Born in Lamar, Missouri

33rd President of the United States

from 1945 to 1953

Previously 34th Vice President from 1944 to 1945

"We have gone a long way toward civilization and religious tolerance, and we have a good example in this country. Here the many protestant denominations, the Catholic Church and the Greek Orthodox Church do not seek to destroy one another in physical violence just because they do not interpret every verse of the Bible in exactly the same way. Here we now have the freedom of all religions, and I hope that never again will we have a repetition of the religious bigotry, as we have had in certain periods of our own history.
There is no room for that kind of foolishness here"

Ivan Turgenev

1818-1883 aged 64

Born in Oryol, Russia

Russian Novelist, Playwright
and Short Story Writer

"Whatever a man prays for,
he prays for a miracle.
every prayer reduces itself to this:
"Great God, grant that twice two
be not four.
Nature is not a temple,
but a workshop,
and man's the workman in it"

Ted Turner

Born 1938 in Cincinnati, Ohio
American Media Mogul
and Major Philanthropist
Founder of CNN
He is One of the Largest US Land Owners
Won the Americas Cup in 1977.
Was Married to Jane Fonda from 1991 to 2001

"Jane just came home and said 'I've become a Christian.'
Before that she was not a religious person.
That's a pretty big change for your wife of
many years to tell you. That's a shock.

Basically we are chimpanzees

with about 2% more intelligence
& a little less hair!"

Archbishop Desmond Tutu

Born 1931 in Klerksdorp, South Africa
South African Activist
First Black Archbishop of Cape Town
Awarded the Nobel Peace Prize in 1984
"When missionaries came to Africa,
they had the Bible and we had the land.
And when they said "Let us pray" we dutifully closed
our eyes, and when we opened them, we had the Bible,
and they had the land!" (Also attributed to Jomo
Kenyatta) "If God is, as they say, homophobic,
I wouldn't worship that God. We struggled against
apartheid in South Africa, supported by people the world
over, because black people were being blamed and made to
suffer for something we could do nothing about; our very
skins...It is the same with sexual orientation.
It is a given"

Cape Town, South Africa

Mark Twain

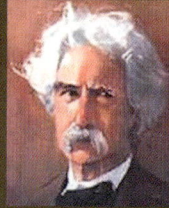

1835-1910 aged 74
Born in Florida Missouri
American Author and Humorist
Printer, Public Speaker and Riverboat Pilot
Most famous for "Tom Sawyer" & "Huckleberry Finn
"To trust the God of the Bible is to trust an irascible,
vindictive, fierce and ever fickle and changeful master.
If Christ were here, there is one thing he would not be - a
Christian. The Bible has noble poetry in it; some clever fables;
and some blood-drenched history; and a wealth of obscenity;
and upwards of a thousand lies. Man is a marvelous
curiosity...he thinks he is the Creator's pet...he even believes
the Creator loves him; yes and watches over him and keeps him
out of trouble, he prays to Him and thinks He listens, Isn't it a
quaint idea. Man is the only Religious Animal. He is the only
animal that has the True Religion—several of them. He is the
only animal that loves his neighbor as himself, and cuts his
throat if his theology isn't straight. A man is accepted into a
church for what he believes, & turned out for what he knows.
Nothing agrees with me.
If I drink coffee it gives me dyspepsia; if I drink wine it gives
me the gout, if I go to church it gives me dysentery. Faith is
believing what you know ain't so. Ignorance is <u>not</u> not
knowin'. Ignorance is knowin' what ain't so.
Go to heaven for the climate, and hell for society"

Mark Twain, continued (Samuel Clemens)

"Truth is more of a stranger than fiction. The so-called Christian nations are the most enlightened and progressive... but in spite of their religion, not because of it, The Church has opposed every innovation and discovery from the day of Galileo down to our own time, when the use of anesthetic in childbirth was regarded as a sin because it avoided the biblical curse pronounced against Eve. And every step in astronomy and geology ever taken has been opposed by bigotry and superstition. The Greeks surpassed us in artistic culture and in architecture, five hundred years before Christian religion was born. There is one notable thing about our Christianity, bad, bloody, merciless, money-grabbing and predatory as it is...it is still a hundred times better than the Christianity of the Bible, with its prodigious crime, the invention of Hell. Measured by our Christianity of today, bad as it is, hypocritical as it is, empty and hollow as it is, neither the Deity nor His Son is a Christian, Ours is a terrible religion. The fleets of the world could swim in spacious comfort, in the innocent blood it has spilt. In religion and politics, people's beliefs and convictions are in almost every case, gotten at second-hand, and without examination, from authorities who have not themselves examined the questions at issue, but have taken them at second-hand from other non-examiners, whose opinions about them are not worth a brass farthing. I cannot see how a man of any large degree of humorous perception, can ever be religious. Most people are bothered by those passages of Scripture they do not understand, but the passages that bother me, are those I do understand. I do not fear death, I was dead for billions of years before I was born, and it never inconvenienced me a bit. Stripping away the irrational, the illogical, and the impossible, I am left with atheism. I can live with that"

John Updike

1932-2009 aged 77
Born in Reading, Pennsylvania
American Novelist, Short Story Writer
Poet, Art Critic and Literary Critic
Won Pulitzer Prizes for Fiction Twice
"In general, the churches, visited by me often
on weekdays...bore for me the same relation to God,
that billboards did to Coca-Cola; they promoted thirst,
without quenching it.
Whenever religion touches science, it gets burned.
In the sixteenth century...astronomy, in the
seventeenth...microbiology, in the eighteenth...geology
and paleontology, in the nineteenth...Darwin's biology,
all grotesquely extended the world- frame and sent
churchmen scurrying for cover in ever smaller, more
shadowy nooks, little ambiguous caves in the psyche,
where even now neurology is cruelly harrying them,
gouging them out from the multifolded brain, like
woodlice from under the wood pile...Only by placing God
on the other side of the humanly understandable, can
any final safety for him be secured.

Sir Peter Ustinov CBE

1921-2004 aged 83
Born in London
English Award Winning Actor, Playwright,
Screenwriter, Director, Filmmaker, Columnist,
Humorist, Broadcaster, TV Presenter, Wit,
Raconteur, Intellectual and Diplomat
"The habit of religion
is oppressive and depressing –
an easy way out of thought.
Beliefs are what divide people.
Doubt unites them.
If Jesus Christ were to come back today,
he would find it virtually impossible to
convince anyone of his credentials, despite the
fact that the vast evangelical machine on
American television, is based on His imminent
return among us sinners"

Vincent van Gogh

1853-1890 aged 37
Born in Groot-Zundert, Netherlands
Dutch, Self-Taught, Post Impressionist
Painter, who Influenced 20th Century Art
With his Vivid Colors & Emotional Impact.
Unappreciated as an Artist,
He Shot Himself When He was Only 37.
He Hardly Sold One Painting in His
Lifetime, Yet Now They Fetch as Much as
$82 Million and more! His Father was a
Dutch Reformed Church Minister

"I can very well do without God both in my
life and in my painting, but I cannot,
suffering as I am, do without something
which is greater than I am, which is my life,
the power to create"

The Vatican

The State of the Vatican City
Was Established in 1929 by Mussolini.
With a Population of Over 800
Its 44 Acres are Walled

Vatican statement in 1866 (The year <u>after</u>
America's Civil War <u>and Slavery</u> Ended)
"Slavery itself ..is not at all contrary to the
natural and divine law..The purchaser of
the slave should carefully examine whether
the slave who is put up for sale, has been
justly or unjustly deprived of his liberty,
and that the vendor should do nothing
which might endanger the life, virtue ,
or Catholic faith of the slave"

Dr Craig Venter

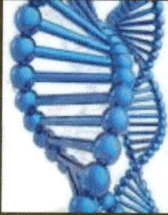

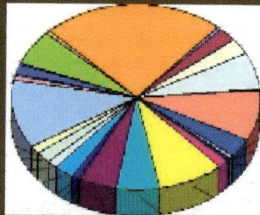

Born 1946 in Salt Lake City, Utah
American Biologist, Entrepreneur,
Researcher, Millionaire Businessman,
Founder of the Institute of Genomic Research,
Decoder of the Human Genome.
In 2005 He Circumnavigated the World,
Researching Marine Microbial Communities
in His Drive to Create New Forms of Life.
Some Consider Him a Genius, Others Call Him
Frankenstein, a Scientist Playing God.

"As an atheist, I think from my experience in
war and life and science, it all has made me
believe that we have one life on this planet.
We have one chance to contribute to the
future of society and the future of life.
The only 'after-life', is what
other people remember of you"

Jesse Ventura

Born 1951 in Minneapolis, Minnesota
Governor of Minnesota from 1999 to 2003
With the Highest Approval Rating
of Any Governor in US History!
Navy Veteran, Professional Wrestler
Actor, Radio & Television Personality

"Organized religion is a sham
and a crutch for weak-minded people who
need strength in numbers. It tells people to go
out and stick their noses in other people's
business. I don't mean all religious people,
but there are lots of people out there
who think they know the truth about
God and religion. But does anybody
really know for sure? I hate what
fundamentalist fanatics
are doing to this country"

Gore Vidal

Born 1925 in West Point, New York
He Died in 2012 in Hollywood Hills, aged 86
Celebrated American Author, Playwright, Screenwriter,
Journalist, Essayist and Liberal Political Activist.
He Wrote more than 30 novels, Many Historical.
Bill Maher Called Him
'America's most interesting man'
"I'm a born-again atheist!

The idea of a good society is something you do not need a religion and eternal punishment to buttress; you need a religion if you are terrified of death. Monotheism is the great unmentionable evil at the centre of our culture...I regard monotheism as the greatest disaster ever to befall the human race. From a barbaric bronze age text known as the Old Testament, three anti-human religions have evolved-Judaism, Christianity and Islam. These are sky-god religions...the sky-god is a jealous god, of course. He requires total obedience from everyone on earth. Although the notion of one god may give comfort to those in need of a daddy, it reminds the rest of us that the totalitarian society is grounded upon the concept of God the father. One God, one King, one Pope, one master in the factory, one father-leader in the family at home.

More people have been killed in the name of Jesus Christ than any other name in the history of the world"

Voltaire

His Chateau Near Lake Geneva   1694-1778 aged 83

Born in Paris, Educated by Jesuits, Exiled to England for 3 Years, Close Friend of Benjamin Franklin.   French Writer, Poet, Playwright, Historian, Novelist, Philosopher and Wit, Civil Liberties Activist, Pro Freedom of Religion & Free Trade.

"Christianity is the most ridiculous, the most absurd, and bloody religion that ever infected the world. Superstition, born of paganism and adopted by Judaism, invested the Christian Church from earliest times. All the fathers of the Church..believed in the power of magic. The Church always condemned magic, but she always believed in it...Nothing can be more contrary to religion and the clergy, than reason and common sense. Every sensible man, every honorable man, must hold the Christian sect in horror. Those who believe absurdities, will commit atrocities. You will notice that in all disputes between Christians...Rome has always favored the doctrine which most completely subjugated the human mind and annihilated reason. The Bible: That is what fools have written, what imbeciles commend, what rogues teach and young children are made to learn by heart. A clergyman is one who feels himself called upon to live without working, at the expense of those who work to live. God created sex, Priests created marriage. On religion, many are destined to reason wrongly, others not to reason at all,
and others to prosecute those who do reason.
Atheism is the voice of a few intelligent people.
I die, as I have lived, a free spirit, an Anarchist,
owing no allegiance to rulers, heavenly or earthly.

Kurt Vonnegut

1922-2007 aged 84
Influential American Writer
"Mother Night" "Slaughterhouse-Five"
"Breakfast of Champions" etc

"My study of anthropology, confirmed my
atheism. Say what you like about the miracle
of unquestioning faith. I consider a capacity
for it terrifying and absolutely vile.
Acceptance of a creed, any creed, entitles the
acceptor to membership in the sort of artificial
extended family we call a congregation.
It's a way to fight loneliness.
I believe that virtuous behavior is trivialized
by carrot-and-stick schemes, such as promises
of highly improbable rewards,
or punishments in an improbable afterlife"

Lalla Ward

Born 1951 in London
Actor, Author and Illustrator
Well Known for Playing Romana
In the BBCTV Series "Dr Who".

As Her First Husband, Tom Baker
Who Played Dr Who, Described Himself as
Irreligious, and She Had a Long Friendship
with "Dr Who" Writer Douglas Adams, Who
was an Atheist, and Remembered for his "The
Hitchhiker's Guide to the Galaxy" and who,
on his 40th Birthday, Introduced Her to the
Most Famous of Atheists: Richard Dawkins
Whom She Married in 1992, and has Co-Read
His Book "The God Delusion"
...It Can Safely be Assumed That She Too
is an Atheist!
(THAT'S NOT A HALO, IT'S A HAT!)

Ibn Warraq

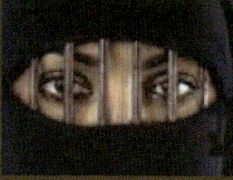

Born 1946 in Pakistan
Was Schooled and Works in Britain
Writer, Speaker And Journalist
Wall Street Journal & The Guardian in London
Author of "Why I Am Not a Muslim"
and "Leaving Islam: Apostates Speak Out"

"Let us face the truth...Islam divides the world in two:
Dar-ul Harb (land of war) and Dar-ul Islam (land of
Islam). Dar-ul Harb is the land of the infidels.
Muslims are required to infiltrate those lands,
proselytize, procreate until their numbers increase, and
then start the war...impose Islam...and convert that
land into Dar-ul Islam... And when the ignorant among
us read those hate-laden verses, they act on them and the
result is September 11, human bombs in Israel, massacres
in East Timor and Bangladesh, kidnappings and killings
in Pakistan and Jordan, torture in Iran, stoning and
maiming in Afghanistan and Iran, violence in Algeria,
terrorism in Palestine and misery and death in
every Islamic country...It is not the extremists who have
misunderstood Islam. They do literally what the Qur'an
asks them to do. It is we who misunderstand Islam"

Lemuel Washburn

Early 20th Century American Secularist Activist
Author of "Is the Bible Worth Reading?" etc

"When Christian ministers stand up in their pulpits and say Let us pray, if they would sometimes vary the invitation and say: LET US LAUGH! they would do their congregations more good. What a queer thing is Christian salvation! Believing in firemen will not save a burning house; but believing in a savior saves men. Fudge! Go into any Christian church and you will hear the choir and the congregation singing lies. Is it not time to stop it? We are told that all things are possible with God, and yet God cannot boil an egg in cold water. Religion is no more the parent of morality than an incubator is the mother of a chicken. An organization that requires the suppression of facts and the discouragement of knowledge in order to maintain its supremacy, is the relic of a tyranny which our free age and our free thought are in duty bound to remove from the earth. The churches erected in the name of God, will ere long be tombstones to his memory. Too long has this world been at the feet of the priest. Man is never in that position for his own benefit, but for the benefit of the priest. If there were no ministers and no priests, how long would there be any churches? Civilization has come about by going to school more than to church. Priest and God have formed one of the worst combinations in history. Have a good time, make life cheerful and bright, dance if you want to, sing if you can, play as long as you live - and leave the world with a smile"

George Washington

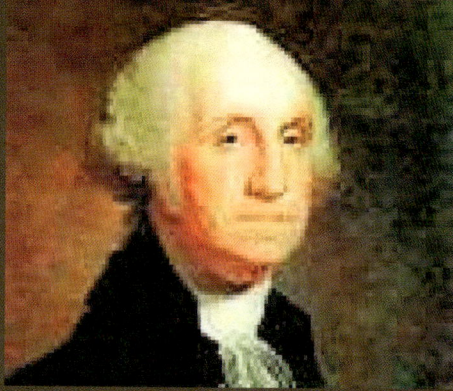

1732 - 1799 aged 67

First President of the United States 1789-1797

He Lead the American Victory Over Great Britain in in the American Revolutionary War, 1775-1787

"The United States of America should have a foundation free from the influence of clergy. As mankind becomes more liberal, they will be more apt to allow that all those who conduct themselves as worthy members of the community, are equally entitled to the protections of civil government. I hope to ever see America among the foremost nations of justice and liberality. There is nothing that can better deserve our patronage than the promotion of science and literature. Knowledge is in every country the surest basis of public happiness. If they are good workmen (for building his Mount Vernon home) they may be from Asia, Africa or Europe; they may be Mahometans, Jews, Christians of any sect, or they may be ATHEISTS"

James Watt

Born 1938 in Lusk, Wyoming
US Secretary of the Interior
Under President Ronald Reagan

"We will mine more,
drill more,
cut more timber.
We don't have to protect
the environment -
the Second Coming
is at hand"

MAY GOD FORGIVE HIM!

Steven Weinberg

Born 1953 in New York City
American Theoretical Physicist
and Nobel Laureate 1979

Science should be taught not in order to support religion, and not in order to destroy religion. Science should be taught simply ignoring religion. Most scientists I know don't care enough about religion, even to call themselves atheists. Good people will do good things, and bad people will do bad things but for good people to do bad things - that takes religion. They felt that science would be corrosive to religious belief, and they worried about it. Damn it, I think they were right! Science is corrosive to religious belief, and it's a good thing! God in the Old Testament, tells us to bash the heads of infidels and demands of us that we be willing to sacrifice our children's lives at His orders, and the God of traditional Christianity and Islam damns us for eternity if we do not worship Him in the right manner. Is this a nice way to behave? I know, I know, we are not supposed to judge God according to human standards. It was the self-righteous true believers who killed Anwar Sadat, Yitzhak Rabin and Mahatma Gandhi"
...AND INDIRA GANDHI AND BENAZIR BHUTTO AND...

Scott D Weitzenhoffer

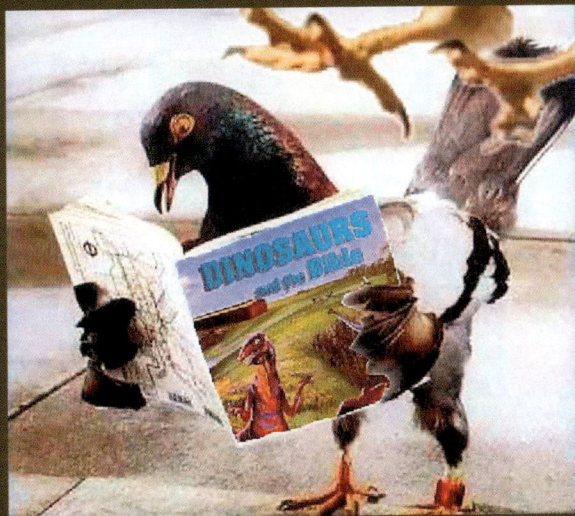

"Debating creationists on the topic
of evolution is rather like trying
to play chess with a pigeon;
it knocks the pieces over,
craps on the board,
and flies back to its flock
to claim victory!"

Tom Weller

Author and Illustrator of
"Science Made Stupid;
How to Discomprehend
the World Around Us"

"Several thousand years ago,
a small tribe of ignorant near-savages
wrote various collections of
myths, wild tales, lies and gibberish.
Over the centuries, these stories were
embroidered, garbled, mutilated
and torn into small pieces
that were then repeatedly shuffled.
Finally, this material was badly translated
into several languages...the resultant text,
creationists feel,
is the best guide to the complex and technical
subject...Creation versus Evolution"

Orson Welles

1915-1985 aged 70

Born in Kenosha, Wisconsin
American Film, Stage and Radio Director
Actor, Producer and Screenwriter, His Films
Include: "Citizen Kane" "Jane Eyre"
"The Magnificent Ambersons" "Othello"
"The Third Man" "Macbeth"
"The Lady From Shanghai"

In 1938 his Halloween Radio Production of
H G Wells' story "The War of the Worlds" caused
some panic, because it was presented so realistically
that many listeners really thought there was
a Martian Invasion!
Some people will believe anything!

"I have a great love and respect for religion,
a great love and respect for atheism.
What I hate is agnosticism, people who do not choose.
I don't pray,
because I don't want to bore God!"

H G Wells

1866-1946 aged 79

Born in Bromley, Kent

English Writer, Historian, Teacher

Journalist, Socialist and Pacifist

He wrote over 100 books, including:

"The Time Machine" "The Invisible Man"

"The Shape of Things to Come"

"The First Man on the Moon"

"The Island of Dr Moreau"

"The War of the Worlds"

After Exposure to Darwinism in School,
He Converted from Devout Christian to
Devout Darwinist. Once He Came to believe in
Evolution, He Could No Longer Accept Genesis.

"All these religions...there they are.
Only they are not true for me...
they do not work for me"

Ella Wheeler Wilcox

1850-1919 aged 69
American Author and Poet
Her Most Famous Work Was
"Poem of Passion"
and Her Most Famous Two Lines are:
'Laugh,
and the world laughs with you,
Weep, and you weep alone'

"So many gods, so many creeds
So many paths that wind and wind,
While just the art of being kind
Is all the sad world needs"

Walt Whitman

1819-1892 aged 72
Born in West Hills, Huntington
Long Island, New York
Journalist, Essayist and Humanist

"God is a mean-spirited,
pugnacious bully, bent on
revenge against His children
for failing to live up to His
impossible standards"

Oscar Wilde

1854-1900 aged 46
Born in Dublin, Ireland
Irish Writer, Playwright, Poet and Wit
He Spoke Throughout America in 1882
Most Famous for His Plays, Between 1892 & 1895
"Lady Windermere's Fan" "An Ideal Husband"
and "The Importance of Being Ernest"
And for His Notorious 1895 Homosexual Trial
His Imprisonment in Reading Jail for Two Years
And His Death, Destitute in Paris.
His last words: "That wallpaper is killing me,
one of us has got to go!"

"When I think of all the harm the Bible has done,
I despair of ever writing anything to equal it.
It is grossly selfish to require of one's neighbour that he
should think in the same way, and hold the same
opinions. Why should he? If he can think, he will
probably think differently. If he cannot think, it is
monstrous to require thought of any kind from him"

Gene Wilder

1933-2005

Born in Milwaukee, Wisconsin
American Award Winning
Stage and Screen Actor
and Screenwriter

"Well
I'm a Jewish -
Buddhist -
Atheist,
I guess!"

Hank Williams Jr

Born 1949 in Shreveport,
Louisiana
American Country Musician
Singer and Songwriter

"I've seen
some preachers on TV.
They say to send your money
to the Lord -
but they give you
their address!"

Tennessee Williams

1911-1983 aged 71
Born in Columbus, Mississippi
Award Winning Playwright
Novelist, Essayist, Poet & Short Story Writer
Renowned for "A Streetcar Named Desire"
"The Glass Menagerie" "Cat on a Hot Tin Roof"
"The Rose Tattoo" "Suddenly, Last Summer"
"The Roman Spring of Mrs Stone"
"Camino Real" etc

"We're all of us guinea pigs
in the laboratory of God.
Humanity is just a work in progress.
All your Western theologies,
the whole mythology of them,
are based on the concept of
God as a senile delinquent"

Bruce Willis

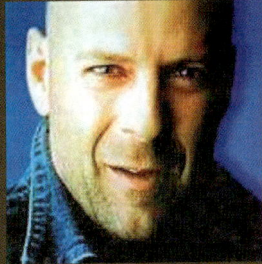

Born 1955 in Idar-Oberstein, West Germany
American Film and TV Actor Producer and Musician.

"Organized religions in general, in my opinion, are dying
forms. They were all very important when we didn't
know why the sun moved, why weather changed, why
hurricanes occurred, or volcanoes happened. Modern
religion is the end trail of modern mythology. But there
are people who interpret the Bible literally.
<u>Literally!</u>
I choose not to believe that's the way,
and that's what makes America cool, you know?

Over the years, I've lost a couple of friends to freak
accidents and it's made me realize how fragile life is, how
quickly it can be taken away. I think about my death
at least once a day and I say to myself 'Am I living my
life to the full? Am I enjoying my life today - right
now?' If the answer is no , then I stop what I'm doing
and do something else. The point is, this is not a
rehearsal. This is it! And I believe that if you are not
appreciating the moment, living in the now,
then you're not doing justice to your own life"

Dr Bird Wilson

American Historian

"The Founding Fathers
of our nation
were nearly all infidels!
Of The Presidents... George
Washington, John Adams, Thomas
Jefferson,
James Madison, James Monroe,
Quincy Adams and Andrew Jackson
...not one professed a belief in
Christianity!"

Woodrow Wilson

1856–1924 aged 68
Born in Staunton, Virginia
28th President of the United States, 1913–1921

"Of course, like every other man of
intelligence and education
I do believe in organic evolution.
It surprises me that at this late date
such questions should be raised.
It does not become America that within
her borders, where every man is free to
follow the dictates of his own conscience,
men should raise the cry of
church against church.
To do so is to strike at the
very heart of America"

Terry Wogan

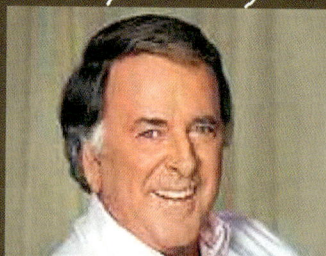

Born 1938 in Limerick, Ireland
London Radio and Television Personality
and Talk Show Host

"I was educated in Ireland under Jesuits
and the worst sin in the Catholic church,
after sex, was vanity! So how any of us
came out of it with any self-regard, I don't
know. But I always had self-esteem. The
Limerick of my childhood was 'cursed' with
religion, breathing fire and brimstone,
telling you how easy it was to sin,
and how you'd be in hell.
We were brainwashed into believing,
and not even the skepticism of my parents -
they knew it was a lot of rubbish -
could protect me from it"

Virginia Woolf

1882-1941 aged 59
Born in London
English Author, Essayist, Publisher
and Short story Writer
Member of the Bloomsbury Group
of Artists, Writers, Intellectuals
and Eccentrics

"I read the Book of Job last night,
I don't think God
comes out well in it"

Frank Lloyd Wright

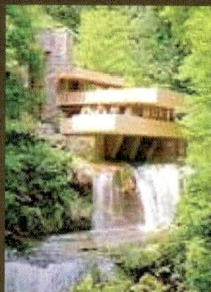

Falling Water

Guggenheim Museum

1887-1959 aged 91
Born in Richland Center, Wisconsin
American Architect,
Interior Designer
Writer and Educator
He Designed Over 1,000 Projects

"I believe in God,
only I spell it
Nature"

Xenophanes

560 BC-478 BC aged 82
Greek Philosopher,
Athenian Thinker Before Socrates

"The clear and perfect truth
no man has seen,
nor will there be any one who
<u>knows</u> about the Gods...
what he says may be,
yet he does not <u>know</u> it.
All things are matters of opinion.
Men imagine gods to be born and to have
clothes and voice and body, like themselves...
If cows and horses had hands and could draw,
cows would draw gods that look like cows,
and horses would draw gods that look like horses.
Ethiopians make their gods black and snub nosed;
Thracians say theirs have blue eyes and red hair.

Thomas Russell Ybarra

1880~1971 aged 91
Born in Caracas, Venezuela
Venezuelan Born American
Journalist and Traveler
"A Christian
Is a man who feels
Repentance on Sunday
For what he did on Saturday
And is going to do on Monday"

Frank Zappa

1940-1993 aged 53
Born in Baltimore, Maryland
Composer, Singer, Songwriter,
Record Producer & Film Director

"Reality is what it is, not what you want it to be.
The essence of Christianity is told us in the
Garden of Eden history. The fruit that was forbidden
was on the tree of knowledge. The subtext is, all the
suffering you have is because you wanted
to find out what was going on.
Then there's Scientology, how about that? You hold on
to the tin cans and then this guy asks you a bunch of
questions, and if you pay enough money you get to join
the master race. How's that for a religion? The
difference between religions and cults is determined by
how much real estate is owned. Change the channel if
you see some guy in a brown suit with a telephone
number at the bottom of the screen, asking for money.
Tax the hell out of the churches! Anyone who wants to
raise a happy, mentally healthy child should keep him
or her as far away from a church as you can!"

Mark Zuckerberg

Born 1984 in White Plains, New York
The World's Youngest Billionaire!
Computer Programmer and
Internet Entrepreneur
Par Excellence!
Educated at Harvard.
Time Magazine's
Person of the Year 2011.
His Net Worth:
Over $13 Billion!
"I consider myself an atheist"
..."AND THE LAST SHALL BE FIRST"! MATTHEW 20.16

AFTERTHOUGHT: All those people who brag that they believe every word of the Bible, that the earth is a mere 6,000 years old, & earliest humans shared the planet with the dinosaurs! I wonder if they have actually read every word of the Bible as I have, or are they in fact, 'Cafeteria Christians', who pick and choose which bits to believe or to take on faith, select a few, really choice, cherry picked, inspiring verses, commit them to memory and leave it at that. When you really stop to think about it all (it seems that thinking is the last thing on their minds)...if the great patriarchs of the Bible were living today...Abraham would be in jail for child abuse and endangerment. Moses would be on trial at The Hague for race hate crimes...causing thousands of Egyptians to drown in the Red Sea, due to parting the waters with reckless disregard for human life. (Didn't Christ say love thine enemies?) Noah might well be facing charges for being in charge of a dangerously overcrowded ferryboat. And Animal Welfare would be on his case for crowding in too many critters in a very confined space for 40 days and 40 nights. Lot would surely be indicted for offering his two lovely daughters to a bunch of rapists for a gang bang. While those same daughters would be found guilty of getting their father drunk in a cave and having sex with him on more than one occasion...a sort of weird date rape. So incest was OK in those days? The Bible certainly conveys some very strange mixed messages. The Blessed Virgin Mary might well, like Martha Stewart, be charged with not telling the whole truth to Federal Agents. Meanwhile, many of the heroes of the of the Old Testament would face multiple counts of ethnic cleansing and crimes against humanity, brought by Amnesty International. And Christ himself would probably find himself in jail and trying to prove his sanity and innocence.   MIKE NEWELL

35625217R20268

Made in the USA
Charleston, SC
12 November 2014